THE COMPLETE IDIOT'S GUIDE® TO

Stock Investing

D0974241

FAST-TRACK

WITHDRAWN

by Ken Little

ALPHA

A member of Penguin Group (USA) Inc.

ALPHA BOOKS

Published by Penguin Group (USA) Inc.

Penguin Group (USA) Inc., 375 Hudson Street, New York, New York 10014, USA • Penguin Group (Canada), 90 Eglinton Avenue East, Suite 700, Toronto, Ontario M4P 2Y3, Canada (a division of Pearson Penguin Canada Inc.) • Penguin Books Ltd., 80 Strand, London WC2R 0RL, England • Penguin Ireland, 25 St. Stephen's Green, Dublin 2, Ireland (a division of Penguin Books Ltd.) • Penguin Group (Australia), 250 Camberwell Road, Camberwell, Victoria 3124, Australia (a division of Pearson Australia Group Pty. Ltd.) • Penguin Books India Pvt. Ltd., 11 Community Centre, Panchsheel Park, New Delhi—110 017, India • Penguin Group (NZ), 67 Apollo Drive, Rosedale, North Shore, Auckland 1311, New Zealand (a division of Pearson New Zealand Ltd.) • Penguin Books (South Africa) (Pty.) Ltd., 24 Sturdee Avenue, Rosebank, Johannesburg 2196, South Africa • Penguin Books Ltd., Registered Offices: 80 Strand, London WC2R 0RL, England

Copyright © 2012 by Ken Little

International Standard Book Number: 978-1-61564-233-5
Library of Congress Catalog Card Number: 2012935357

14 13 12   8 7 6 5 4 3 2 1

Interpretation of the printing code: The rightmost number of the first series of numbers is the year of the book's printing; the rightmost number of the second series of numbers is the number of the book's printing. For example, a printing code of 12-1 shows that the first printing occurred in 2012.

Printed in the United States of America

Note: This publication contains the opinions and ideas of its author. It is intended to provide helpful and informative material on the subject matter covered. It is sold with the understanding that the author and publisher are not engaged in rendering professional services in the book. If the reader requires personal assistance or advice, a competent professional should be consulted.

The author and publisher specifically disclaim any responsibility for any liability, loss, or risk, personal or otherwise, which is incurred as a consequence, directly or indirectly, of the use and application of any of the contents of this book.

Most Alpha books are available at special quantity discounts for bulk purchases for sales promotions, premiums, fundraising, or educational use. Special books, or book excerpts, can also be created to fit specific needs. For details, write: Special Markets, Alpha Books, 375 Hudson Street, New York, NY 10014.

Publisher: *Mike Sanders*

Executive Managing Editor: *Billy Fields*

Senior Acquisitions Editor: *Brook Farling*

Development Editor: *Mark Reddin*

Senior Production Editor: *Janette Lynn*

Copy Editor: *Tricia Liebig*

Cover Designer: *Kurt Owens*

Book Designers: *William Thomas, Rebecca Batchelor*

Indexer: *Brad Herriman*

Layout: *Ayanna Lacey*

Proofreader: *John Etchison*

To my daughter Emma, an aspiring writer, who is a better writer now at age 15 than many adults. Here's hoping she writes a best-seller and can take care of her mother and me in my old age.

Contents

Introduction

Investing in the stock market can seem like venturing to a foreign country where the inhabitants speak a language you don't understand. People are shouting numbers and terms that are meaningless to you. Screens flash, letters and numbers scroll across endlessly, and it seems to be utter chaos.

Welcome to Wall Street.

The world you see on cable television and buzzing around the internet is only part of the picture. This part of Wall Street is dedicated to stock market traders, and every market move up is cause for celebration and every move down cause for alarm.

The other part of Wall Street is quiet, calm, and logical. It's where you find long-term investors who buy great companies at great prices and let them build wealth over time. When you become a resident of this world, you realize that about 98 percent of the daily noise surrounding stocks is meaningless to long-term investors.

This book is for long-term investors and describes how you can identify, analyze, and buy great companies at great prices. Long-term investors buy companies, so most of your work will be valuing companies, not stocks. If analyzing a business seems impossible, not to worry. Thanks to the internet, virtually everything you need to analyze companies is free or available for a small price.

Is it easy to pick great stocks? No, it is not, but it is also not impossibly hard either. It takes work, patience, and an understanding of the process, which is where this book comes in. I've boiled the process down to its essentials. When you understand the essentials, you are ready to begin. As you work through the process, you will gain confidence and learn more about the benefits of long-term investing.

Warren Buffett became a billionaire many times over by buying great companies at great prices and letting them make him rich over time. Will you make a billion dollars using this book's essentials? Probably not—however, if you do, remember who got you started. I do hope what you learn here helps you build an investment plan to reach your financial goals.

You might want to check out my two websites:

- Stocks.about.com, where I write about investing in stocks
- Yourmoneyin60seconds.com, where I write about investing in general

Fast-Track Extras

Throughout this book, you will find sidebars with extra information that will further your understanding of the topic at hand. They appear as follows:

DEFINITION

These explain key terms relevant to investing in stocks.

STOCK TIP

Look to these for insight to help you reach your investment goals.

MARKET RISK

These will alert you to common pitfalls and risky moves related to stock investing.

Acknowledgments

Many thanks to the fine folks at Alpha for all their hard work on this book: Brook Farling, Mark Reddin, Janette Lynn, and Tricia Liebig. It is a much better book than what I submitted and I am grateful for their suggestions, corrections, and general shepherding of this project.

Trademarks

All terms mentioned in this book that are known to be or are suspected of being trademarks or service marks have been appropriately capitalized. Alpha Books and Penguin Group (USA) Inc. cannot attest to the accuracy of this information. Use of a term in this book should not be regarded as affecting the validity of any trademark or service mark.

The Basics

Investing in stocks can seem complicated and overwhelming. If you believe the hype, you might think that only a select few are capable of being successful investing in stocks. This is wrong thinking. Investing in stocks is not something you do without some preparation and some homework, but if you're willing to put in some effort it can be a rewarding way to meet your financial goals. Indeed, owning stocks may be the only way to meet your goals.

Let's begin with a brief overview of stocks and why you should consider using them to meet your financial goals. If you are familiar with stocks already, please don't skip this chapter, because you may find some of the things you believe about stocks are wrong. It will also serve to help you focus on those things that are really important.

What Is a Stock?

Common stocks, also known as equities, represent a unit of ownership in a publicly traded corporation. Each share of stock comes with certain rights such as a vote at the annual meeting on important corporation matters. Because you are an owner of the corporation, it is important that you pay attention to the financial and market news concerning the company you own.

This book focuses on investing in individual stocks as one part of a complete investment program. Your investment program should consist of stocks, bonds, and cash. This focus on stocks will allow you the tools to identify great companies. But you can also own stocks through investment vehicles other than individual ownership. The most common ways are through mutual funds and exchange traded funds. It is likely that many of you will own both individual stocks and stocks through mutual funds or exchange traded funds.

STOCK TIP

Although owning stocks through mutual funds and exchange traded funds has some advantages, it is usually more expensive than buying individual stocks. However, many investors use several investment types to meet their goals.

Prices in Stock Markets

The stock market, or markets as they are collectively known, price stocks on a daily basis. The markets, which are mostly electronic, match buyers and sellers, theoretically creating an efficient process that prices equities correctly. Stock prices are determined by the forces of supply and demand in the market on a daily basis. However, the price of stock is strongly correlated to its value as an ongoing business. Even though other factors such as economic news may affect stock prices on a daily basis, the price will generally reflect how the market values the company.

Companies that show superior economic performance command the highest stock prices over the long term. However, the stock market is not always right. Clever investors will spot companies that are undervalued (underpriced) and take advantage of the opportunity to buy with the faith that at some point the markets will correctly value the stock and the investor will profit.

Rights of Ownership

Common stock carries with it some rights and privileges that are important to individual investors. You have a right to vote at the annual meeting either in person or by mail and you have a right to bring issues before the annual meeting that concern you about the company or company policies. In truth, only large investors (usually mutual funds, insurance companies, pension funds, and others that own millions of shares) are really listened to at annual meetings, although by law every stockholder has certain rights to bring issues before the meeting that the company cannot deny. However, if you own stock in a company that is having an annual meeting nearby, I encourage you to attend just to see how they are run. Actually getting into the meeting is usually not as simple as showing up, so investigate what type of credentials you will need.

Some companies pay a portion of their profits to stockholders in the form of dividends. While not all companies pay dividends, those that do are often attractive investments especially for individuals in need of current income, such as retirees.

The decision to pay a dividend and the amount is up to the board of directors. Dividends are usually paid on a quarterly basis and may be increased, decreased, or eliminated by the board of directors as it sees fit.

Preferred stock trades separately from common stock. However, the real value of owning preferred shares is that they receive preferential treatment for dividends. In fact, about the only reason to own preferred shares is for the dividend. Some industries such as utilities, for example, are known for paying consistent and strong dividends.

 DEFINITION

> **Preferred stock** is considered a special class of stock. Owners are paid dividends before common stockholders and have preferred rights to assets in the event of bankruptcy or liquidation. However, preferred stockholders can't vote at annual meetings.

Why Invest in Stocks?

Historically, stocks have proven to be one of the most success-ful long-term investments that most people can make. The key phrase here is "long-term" because all of us have experienced dramatic up-and-down swings in the stock market. If you want to invest in individual stocks, plan on holding them for a long period, if possible.

Long-Term Growth Potential

Over the history of stocks, going back 90 years or so, investors have realized an average annual return of somewhere between 8 and 10 percent, depending on how the returns were calcu-lated. That return is qualified with the understanding that it is reflective of the broad stock market, not individual stocks. Some individual stocks have failed miserably and indeed companies have gone bankrupt, which makes the stock worthless, and other companies have returned much more than the average to its investors.

The concept of buying stocks and holding them for a long period is known as "buy and hold" investing. Hotshots on the internet and in infomercials often deride this form of investing. However, it is a proven strategy that works if you pay attention to what's happening with the company and make adjustments as the company changes over time. Buy-and-hold does not mean buy and be stupid. If the company no longer reflects the superior economics that led you to buy it in the first place, it is probably time to sell and move on to something else. If you are paying attention, you'll probably notice the decline beginning and sell before the stock's price is dramatically affected.

Easy Buying and Selling

One of the most attractive features of owning individual stocks is that they are easy to buy and sell. Except for national holidays and weekends, the stock market creates a liquid market that will match buyers and sellers.

Because it is easy to buy and sell individual stocks, some investors are tempted into trading frequently in an attempt to profit on price changes. While there are people who make money doing this, they are professional investors who, for the most part, spend a great deal of time watching prices on the stock market. For the casual trader who jumps in and out of the market trying to time price changes, the end is almost always a significant loss of money.

Unlike some other investment opportunities, the *liquidity* of individual stocks means you can almost certainly sell your stock when you want to. However, there is no guarantee you will always get the price you want, especially if you have to sell because of a sudden change in your financial position or a sudden change with the company.

 DEFINITION

Liquidity refers to the ease an investor can convert an asset to cash. Stock, mutual funds, and bank CDs are liquid, while real estate is illiquid.

Important Part of Investment Plan

Stocks are an important part of every investment plan. It is hard to imagine an investment strategy that could be successful over the long term without stocks as an essential part of the strategy.

Investors often combine stocks with bonds and cash to create a more balanced investment plan. Bonds, which are debt securities issued by government entities or corporations, frequently move in the opposite direction of stocks. If equities are generally up, it is common that bonds will decline in value. This relationship helps investors benefit no matter which way the stock market is moving. While bonds may provide balance to the volatility sometimes present in the stock market, during the long term it is the stocks that will provide the greatest return.

Buying the Business, Not the Stock

A significant part of this book is devoted to examining and analyzing businesses. This may come as a surprise to many new investors, who may have expected to be examining stocks. However, investors make money in the stock market by buying great companies, not great stocks.

Investing in stocks is really about investing in businesses. Don't be intimidated at the thought of analyzing businesses when balancing the checkbook is a struggle enough. The good news is that most of the heavy lifting has already been done by people more qualified than you or I to crunch the numbers.

It is important, however, that you understand the key metrics and how you can use them to make decisions about buying or selling a stock. You will put as much effort into deciding when to sell as you will in deciding when to buy. Chapter 3 will begin this process by identifying those sources that will help you in your investigations.

Relating a Company's Value to Stock Price

On a daily basis, the stock market can be extremely volatile, meaning there are big swings in prices, especially in those stocks that are frequently traded. The real value of a company is not necessarily reflected in the daily price fluctuations of its stock.

Frequent changes in economic data such as unemployment, economic growth, interest rates, and so on can cause stock prices to go up or down in reaction. While some of these changes can have a long-term impact on the value of the business, many factors that drive daily stock prices up or down have little affect long term on the economic health of a company.

Your job as an investor is to judge whether changes in economic or market conditions will have a long-term affect on the company's value. You don't have to be an economist to figure this out, but you do have to do your homework, which means keeping up-to-date with the major economic and market trends.

Buying Great Companies

There are a number of ways to define great companies. For example, some companies make tremendous products and feature glamorous advertisements that are very attractive to consumers. However, their financial health may not be the best. A common mistake in investing is to buy stock in a company you admire. While there's nothing wrong with investing in companies that you have an emotional connection with, it is important that you not let emotions cloud your judgment.

Great companies, for the purpose of this book, are organizations that consistently return value to their owners. In some cases, value can be the stock price that grows faster than the market in general. It can also be defined as companies that consistently pay a reasonable dividend.

These great companies will make up the core of your investing program. However, you can also find great companies that are defined by their potential. Frequently, companies like this are small, but have exceptional growth potential. While they won't have a long history of financial success, you will be able to determine a value and assess their long-term growth potential.

Avoiding Greed and Fear

There are two primary emotions that spell trouble for investors in the stock market: greed and fear. Both of these emotions drive investors to make irrational and invariably wrong decisions. Greed becomes apparent when investors believe a stock or group of stocks is poised for rapid growth. If tech stocks are up, then you should be buying tech stocks. The problem with this thinking is that buying decisions are not grounded in any rational examination of the value of tech stocks.

Most of us remember the tech boom and bust that saw stock prices rise dramatically beyond any sense of rational analysis. Greed drove prices higher and higher until even the most aggressive buyers realized they were not sustainable. When that happened, fear seized the market and most investors sold their tech stocks for any price they could get. More recently, the real estate bubble that burst in 2008 and the resulting financial crisis almost destroyed our economy. Even though these examples may seem isolated, the same bad decisions that created the tech bubble and the real estate fiasco are made every day in the stock market. You can insulate yourself from many of these problems by investing based on a strategy that avoids fads and trends. Stick with great companies that you monitor on a regular basis and you will avoid many of these mistakes.

You will know it is time to buy or sell rather than looking to the market to follow other investors whose buying and selling decisions may be driven more by greed or fear than rational thought.

MARKET RISK

Fear of loss is a powerful emotion. If you invest in stocks, you will, at some time, suffer a loss. If the thought of losing money makes your stomach hurt, maybe investing in the stock market is not for you. If you can't learn from your loss and move on, stick with safer investments.

Taking the Long View

Investing in stocks can be an important strategy to reach your financial goals. If you buy great companies, you will find that holding them for the long term is a very rewarding strategy. However, if you have a financial goal that must be met in fewer than five years, you'll need to find another investment vehicle besides stocks to reach that goal. Over a period shorter than five years, stocks can be very volatile, which places your short-term financial goals in jeopardy.

Investing for the Long Term

Your single most important financial goal is a retirement nest-egg and wisely investing in great companies will help you prepare for a financially secure retirement. As you approach retirement age it is important to recognize the volatile nature of stocks over the short term and begin unwinding your stock positions into something more stable such as cash or bonds. In Chapter 9, I talk about different portfolio mixes and how those change as you approach retirement.

Investing for the long term takes patience and a willingness to stand by your investment decisions even when others disagree. This confidence comes with experience and a continuing education in understanding how to recognize great companies. If you have done your homework and are confident in your conclusion, don't be swayed by other opinions. The reason successful long-term investors continually review the great companies they own is to spot changes that may signal time to move on. This diligence builds confidence that allows you to change your mind based on facts and research, not guesses or tips from others.

The Market Moves in Mysterious Ways

Long-term investors face a constant challenge from the stock market that seems, at times, to move in a random and unpredictable fashion. In times of true economic crisis, you would expect the stock market to decline rapidly. This was certainly true during the 2008 financial crisis precipitated by a collapse of the housing market, among other factors.

When the market appears to be in free fall, it is tempting to do what many others are doing and dump all of your stocks in favor of cash or bonds. More often than not, that is exactly the wrong thing to do. If you still believe you own great companies, but it is difficult to watch share prices decline with the market, what should you do? The best strategy is to sit tight. Historically, investors who ride out dips in the market recover in a better position than those to flee a falling market and buy back into a rising market (sell low, buy high).

Long-term investors need courage to stick it out through the market's invariable rollercoaster rides. If you have done your homework, you will have the confidence to hold on to your great companies. By the way, market dips can be good times to add to your holdings at bargain prices.

Establishing a Plan

Investing in stocks is an important part of achieving your financial goals. The importance of planning for your financial goals extends beyond the obvious and helps you choose the right stock for each goal. Matching investment strategies and financial products produces the best chance for success. Stocks are one of many tools you can use; however, the historical significance of investing in a diversified stock portfolio suggests that you may have a more difficult time achieving your goals without the inclusion of stocks.

Investment Goals

We all have financial goals, whether it's a retirement nest-egg, college for the kids, a down-payment for a new house, or all of the above. You may have other financial goals beyond these. I hope you have written these goals down in specific terms with dollar amounts and dates for completion. Specific goals with specific dates (I want $50,000 in the college fund by the time my daughter reaches 18) will help you focus on achieving your plan. More importantly, having specific goals and dates will help you decide how stocks are going to help you achieve the goals.

Major Financial Goals

Retirement planning is the most important financial goal, because it involves the most money and needs the most time to achieve. If you are 25 years old, retirement is probably the last thing on your mind. However, if you are 50 years old, a healthy retirement nest-egg becomes a much more urgent concern. The irony is you would not worry about having a robust retirement fund at age 50 if you had started at age 25.

Regardless of your age, major financial goals are what shape the decisions you make about investing in the stock market. While a complete financial plan includes more than stocks, if you don't get that part right, the other financial products you use will not likely make up the difference.

Timing of Your Goals

The two key parts of your investment plan are goals and anticipated completion dates. Investing in stocks for these goals is driven by both elements, however timing is the most important element. Stocks are your best chance for investing success over the long term. As I noted in Chapter 1, there are several ways to invest in stocks. I believe the case for using individual stocks as your primary investment tool (as opposed to mutual funds and exchange traded funds), is solid with all the caveats noted in this book.

The use of individual stocks for long-term investing is well-founded, however short-term trading strategies (gambling, really) are not, as you will see in the sections that follow. The record is clear that most people who try to time the market through short-term trading fail. What you want is a long-term strategy that gives you the best opportunity to achieve your financial goals.

MARKET RISK

The internet is full of businesses that want to do you a favor and give you the secrets of successful investing. Avoid get-rich-quick schemes that promise a way to quit your job after you make a killing in the market. There are no secrets to investing success except hard work and a long-term view.

When to Avoid Stocks

Investing in stocks is not always the best answer for a financial goal. There are times when you should use other products besides stocks. Investing in stocks to meet short-term goals is usually not a good idea. I recommend you do not use stocks for any goal that is fewer than five years from completion. Any financial goal you need to achieve in fewer than five years is exposed to a risk that the stock market will swing to the downside just when you need the money.

For example, if you have $30,000 saved for a down-payment on a house and you anticipate buying within the next five years, move that money out of the stock market and into an investment that will secure your principal for the next five years. You can use a bank CD, a U.S. Treasury bond, or some other safe investment so when it comes time for the down-payment you know the $30,000 will still be there. Stocks cannot provide that security. This example assumes you have made allowances for current and anticipated inflation, taxes, and other expenses. The point is that even the best plans can be sabotaged by a volatile stock market over the short term.

As you approach retirement, you will want to dial back your exposure to stocks and move into safer alternatives. I'll talk more about this in Chapter 9.

Investment Strategy

Every investor needs an investment strategy; however, you don't need to be a Wall Street whiz to develop your own. It takes knowing how the basic strategies work, the stocks that are appropriate for that strategy, and an understanding of the risks and potential rewards of investing in stocks. Fortunately, we live in an age when access to important information about companies and stocks is literally at your fingertips. I'll cover how you can find the information you need to make these decisions in Chapter 3.

You will also find thousands of people on the internet who will be glad to share their strategies with you (for free or not). Unfortunately, many of these strategies are really trading schemes that involve a lot of complicated maneuvers and sophisticated products (selling naked calls, for example). I doubt that many investors who buy into these plans understand the risks involved. You will find many well-meaning people who have an investment strategy they will share for free. Some of these homegrown strategies may actually work, at least in some market conditions. Be careful accepting investment advice from anyone (that's one reason I don't recommend an individual stock or any other financial product).

 DEFINITION

Naked calls are an example of very risky investments. In this case, you sell a call option, which gives the owner the right to buy a stock at a set price regardless of the current market price, on a stock you do not own. If the owner of the call option exercises the option, you must buy the stock on the open market and sell it to the option owner at the price of the call, which will be less than you paid. In other words, you take a loss (usually big).

Your investment strategy will work best if you build it yourself using the guidance I provide in this book. This basic strategy will help you begin investing in stocks and if you want to learn more (and you should), there are other books and many websites that you can use. Your investment plan will use one or more of the three basic strategies:

- Investing for growth
- Investing for safety
- Balanced investing

I cover the types of stocks used in these three strategies in Chapter 5.

Investing for Growth Strategy

A growth investing strategy seeks to grow your money (capital) over a long period. The goal is to identify stocks that will provide better than average capital gains (stock price appreciation). In other words, you are looking for *growth stocks* that can be bought at a reasonable price and with a level of risk that is appropriate for you.

Growth investing can be more risky than other strategies. If you understand the risk associated with different types of growth stocks, you can set your own level of risk. There is much more about growth stocks and risk in Chapter 5.

Investing for Safety Strategy

As the name suggests, investing for safety is a conservative approach to growing your money. An investing for safety strategy is focused more on protecting capital (not losing money) and less on growth. Each investor will need to determine exactly where their comfort level (or risk tolerance, if you prefer) is and formulate an investing strategy that accommodates those guidelines.

As some point, many investors will use an investing for safety strategy for all or part of their goals. A person nearing retirement is an obvious example—the need to preserve capital outweighs the need for growth. *Core stocks* may appeal to you for reasons outlined in Chapter 5 (in short they represent solid, large companies that are the foundation of many investment strategies). *Value stocks*, which I discuss in detail in Chapter 5 as well, tend to be less volatile than growth stocks and may be a part of your safety strategy.

 DEFINITION

Growth stocks, while potentially risky, appreciate faster than the market as a whole and provide the best opportunity for significant long-term gains. **Core stocks** represent the largest and most stable companies. They may not register high growth, but they are the most stable, especially when the market is volatile. **Value stocks** are underpriced market bargains to be sold when their true worth is reflected in the price per share.

Balanced Investing Strategy

Investors, depending on their age and risk tolerance, often choose an investment strategy that is a blend of growth and safety, which I call balanced investing. This investment strategy recognizes the need for growth to reach major financial goals, while providing a degree of safety to offset the turbulence that can accompany growth investing.

A truly balanced investment strategy includes bonds or other fixed-income products and cash in appropriate proportions. However, because this book is about stocks, I'll stick to examining how investors can balance that portion of the investment formula.

Think of a balanced stock strategy as an engine that propels your investments toward your financial goals. Growth stocks are the accelerator while safety stocks (core and value) are the brakes. As you change the mix between the accelerator and the brakes, you speed up (more growth stocks) or slow down (more safety stocks) your progress. Also as with a car, the faster you go (more growth stocks), the greater the chance for an accident—another way to say more risk. Likewise, if you stomp on the brakes (safety stocks), you may not reach your destination.

That's as far as I want to go with the car analogy, but it illustrates how growth and safety stocks work together. When you build a balanced investment strategy you decide on the proper mix of growth and safety. As you grow older, and have life-changing events (marriage, children, and so forth), you need to change the mix. Because life is never quite this simple, you will undoubtedly have several investment strategies for your major financial goals. After you understand the various strategies, the different types of stocks, and how they all fit together, you will be ready to shape your strategies.

Risk and Reward

Investing in stocks (or almost anything else) entails taking some risk. There is no investing in stocks without risk and there is no return without risk. That is absolutely the most important truth you need to understand when formulating an investment strategy. If you are adverse to the idea of taking any amount of risk, then stocks are not for you. It will be more difficult (but not impossible) for you to reach your financial goals without investing in stocks.

One of the most important and often misunderstood considerations in shaping an investment strategy is the relationship of risk and potential reward in stock investing.

Understanding Risk

Risk is the potential for your investment to lose money, for a variety of reasons—meaning your stock's price will fall below what you paid for it. No one wants to lose money on an investment, but there's a good chance you will if you invest in stocks. This is why your investment strategy must contain guidelines for buying and selling the stocks.

The rule of thumb is "the higher the risk, the higher the potential return," but you need to consider an addition to the rule so that it states the relationship more clearly: the higher the risk, the higher the potential return, and the less likely it will achieve the higher return.

Buying a stock that is risky doesn't mean you will lose money and it doesn't mean it will achieve a 25 percent gain in one year. However, both outcomes are possible. How do you know what the risk is and how do you determine what the potential reward (stock price gain) should be?

STOCK TIP

Financial websites report key ratios for stocks and you can use that information to gauge how risky they are. While these scores change with time, they are a good starting point to help you understand and identify various types of risks.

Measuring Risk Against Reward

When you evaluate stocks as potential investment candidates, you should come up with an idea of what the risks are and how much of a potential price gain would make the risks acceptable. Calculating risk and potential reward is as much an art as it is a science. Fortunately, there are a number of websites that have done much of the work for you, but you still need to understand the principle of risk and reward to make an educated investment as opposed to a guess.

The most common type of risk is the danger your investment will lose money. You can make investments that guarantee you won't lose money, but you will give up most of the opportunity to earn a return in exchange. When you calculate the effects of inflation and the taxes you pay on the earnings, your investment may return very little in real growth.

Will I Achieve My Financial Goals?

The elements that determine whether you achieve your investment goals are the following:

- Amount invested
- Length of time invested
- Rate of return or growth
- Fewer fees, taxes, and inflation

If you can't accept much risk in your investments, then you will earn a lower return as noted in the previous section. To compensate for the lower anticipated return, you must increase the amount invested and the length of time it is invested. Many investors find that a modest amount of risk in their portfolio is an acceptable way to increase the potential of achieving their financial goals. By diversifying their portfolio with investments of various degrees of risk, they hope to take advantage of a rising market and protect themselves from dramatic losses in a down market.

Minimize Risk—Maximize Reward

The most successful investment is one that gives you the most return for the least amount of risk. Every investor needs to find his or her comfort level with risk and construct an investment strategy around that level. A portfolio that carries a significant degree of risk may have the potential for outstanding returns, but it also may fail dramatically.

Your comfort level with risk should pass the "good night's sleep" test, which means you should not worry about the amount of risk in your portfolio so much as to lose sleep over it.

There is no "right or wrong" amount of risk—it is a very personal decision for each investor. However, young investors can afford higher risk than older investors can because young investors have more time to recover if disaster strikes. If you are five years away from retirement, you don't want to be taking extraordinary risks with your nest-egg, because you will have little time left to recover from a significant loss. Of course, a too-conservative approach may mean you don't achieve your financial goals.

Having Reasonable Expectations

Unreasonable expectations of how your portfolio should perform can lead to poor decisions, such as taking more risk to make up the difference between your expectations and reality. What is an unreasonable expectation? Expecting to gain 25 percent per year when the broader market is returning 8 percent is unreasonable. Expecting your portfolio to not fall when the market is down 35 percent is unreasonable.

What is a reasonable expectation of portfolio performance? As consultants are fond of saying, "it depends." If your stocks are more heavily weighted toward growth, it is not unreasonable to expect to do better than an index of the broader market that is more heavily weighted toward growth. For example, the Russell 1000 is a broad-based index based on large growth stocks. If your portfolio is heavily weighted to large growth stocks, this index would provide a useful measure to judge your portfolio's performance. The sources I discuss in Chapter 3 have a lot of information on such indexes to help you determine what would be a reasonable expectation for your portfolio. This assumes, of course, that you built the portfolio with certain goals in mind and made your choices based on logical analysis.

When investors fall behind in reaching financial goals, the temptation is to become more aggressive, which leads to unreasonable expectations. If you choose more risky stocks (young technology companies, for example), you may have some winners that will help make up lost ground, but the odds are higher that you will simply fall farther behind. The stock market and the economy don't care about your goals or investment choices. They move due to a variety of factors and will go up or down with no regard to your plans. When the market is rising, your portfolio should also rise (and perhaps a little faster) and when the market falls, your portfolio should not drop as far or as fast. That's the best you can hope for and if you hit it, you are ahead of the game, as they say.

Types of Risk

There are two major types of stock market risks for stock investors: systematic and nonsystematic risks. It is important that you understand that your stocks may go down in price based on risks you have no control over. However, even though you don't have control of these risks, you can prepare for them and provide some protection for your portfolio.

The other major type of risk to your portfolio is when you make unwise investment decisions, such as not doing your homework, paying too much for stock, investing on a tip, and so on.

Systematic Risks

Systematic risks are those issues that affect the stock market and/ or the economy. These types of risk generally hurt all types of stocks, although some stocks may be more susceptible to some risks than others are. Systematic risks include the following:

Economic risk. One of the most obvious risks of investing is that the economy can go bad. Following the market bust in 2000 and the terrorists' attacks in 2001, the economy settled into a sour spell. A combination of factors saw the market indexes lose significant percentages. It took years to return to levels close to pre-9/11 marks, only to have the bottom fall out again in 2008 and 2009 during the financial crisis.

Inflation risk. Inflation is the tax on everyone. It destroys value and creates recessions. Inflation is when too much money chases too few goods. The result is sharply rising prices that are not matched by increases in consumer income. This devalues money.

Historically, stocks have been a good hedge against inflation because companies can raise prices and pass them on to consumers. However, if consumers slow their buying, companies have too much inventory and begin closing manufacturing and retail facilities. The resulting slowing of the economy hurts company value and stock prices decline. Often a recession follows periods of high inflation.

Market value risk. Market value risk refers to what happens when the market turns against or ignores your investment. It also happens when the market collapses—good stocks as well as bad stocks suffer as investors stampede out of the market. Some investors view it as an opportunity to load up on great stocks at a time when the market isn't bidding up the price. On the other hand, it doesn't advance your cause to watch your investment flat-line month after month while other parts of the market are going up.

Geopolitical risk. We live in a global market. Political changes in other countries can adversely affect the U.S. markets. Most of the companies in the S&P 500 Index (the top 500 U.S. companies) make a substantial portion of their sales in countries other than the United States. This makes our stock market vulnerable to political or economic unrest with our global trading partners.

Nonsystematic Risks

Nonsystematic risks are those particular to a company or a small group of companies rather than the whole stock market. You can't protect yourself completely from these risks; however, considering the quality of management in your evaluation may help to minimize the risks, as well as build a diversified portfolio. Examples of nonsystematic risks include the following:

Poor management decisions. Managing a business is a complex job, and the larger the business, the more complex decision-making becomes. A very real risk is that managers will make poor decisions and those decisions will decrease the value of the company.

Most managers act in good faith and believe they are doing what is best for the company and its stockholders. However, managers sometimes just get it wrong and other times act out of motives that are not in the best interest of the company or the stockholders. Spending time reviewing the key managers is an important part of evaluating a company.

Narrow sector factors. Sometimes an economic or market blip will hit a narrow sector of stocks. An example of this is when many years ago, the government imposed a steep tax on luxury items. Almost overnight the luxury boat-building industry in the United States dipped dramatically. Another time during a domestic oil boom, the government imposed an excessive profits tax at the wellhead. You can imagine how that affected oil producers. Sometimes the problem is the result of unintended consequences. The market for inexpensive point-and-shoot digital cameras continues to suffer as more consumers buy smart phones, which all have built-in cameras.

STOCK TIP

You may not be able to avoid nonsystematic risks, but you can reduce their threat by doing your homework and taking care when evaluating companies. In addition to careful evaluation of individual companies, a diversified portfolio will provide protection from nonsystematic risks.

Minimizing Risks

The best protection is a portfolio with the appropriate ratio of stocks, bonds, and cash. I'll focus on the stock portion of that equation. Some systematic and nonsystematic risks have no protection from the portfolio losses they cause. A major recession like the one that began in 2008 is probably going to hurt every stock you own. However, there are steps you can take to reduce or minimize losses from these risks.

Don't invest all of your capital in the same stock sectors, and diversify by size. Own some (not more than 10 percent) foreign stocks to help offset problems caused in the domestic economy. I discuss building portfolios that vary from aggressive to conservative in Chapter 9. These strategies will help you avoid some of the market risks facing all stock investors.

The Traps of Trading— Your Biggest Risk

Market timing may be the two most dangerous words in investing, especially when practiced by beginners. Market timing is the strategy of attempting to predict future price movements through use of various fundamental and technical analysis tools. At its best, market timing is a risky business for professional investors. The real danger exists for beginners who are tempted by what looks like easy money. All you have to do is buy a stock today and sell it tomorrow for a "gut feeling it was going up." Yes, this happens every once in a while, but somebody has to win the lottery, too (here's a hint: it won't be you or me).

Professional traders use highly sophisticated trading techniques driven by computer programs that analyze huge volumes of data almost instantly. You are competing with them when you attempt to play the trading game, and you will probably lose. Professional traders have a name for amateurs who believe they can win: "dumb money." With all of their technology and huge bankrolls behind them, not even all professional traders are successful for an extended period.

Finding and Understanding Information

The best and most reliable sources for financial information are on the internet. No other resource offers you the depth and breadth of information that is available virtually instantly and at no cost to you. You can find the same basic information in documents from the regulatory reports that companies must file; however, it is difficult to wade through the detail to find the "must know" information.

A number of websites go beyond the regulatory filings and compute financial ratios and other metrics. Equally important, you can compare companies with peers and market indexes. You can analyze companies to a degree that would've been impossible before the internet without spending hours poring over documents and doing your own calculations.

The real problem is not a lack of information, but too much information for many people. Sorting through all the websites that offer company information, or even one website, can be confusing and disheartening unless you know what to look for. The most important tool investors need to master is the stock screen, which will help identify companies worthy of more research.

Finding Information on the Internet

Finding information on the internet is easy if you know where to look and where not to look. Clearly, some resources are better than others for information on specific companies. An obvious starting point for many people will be Google (or other search engines such as Bing), the ubiquitous search engine that finds everything. Although search engines can be helpful, you will save time by going directly to key information sources.

I have several suggestions for reputable sources that offer tools to help you manage information, as well as find it. I also have some suggestions about how to avoid content that is biased and seeks to promote a particular product, such as a stock picking service. Later in this chapter, I introduce you to stock screens. If you are not already a user of these helpful assistants, you are in for a pleasant surprise.

 MARKET RISK

> The problem with using search engines such as Google is that you get too much information and websites ranked near the top may or may not be good resources. However, search engines can be helpful if you are looking for a specific answer such as: What were IBM's earnings last quarter?

Morningstar

Morningstar (morningstar.com) is one of the best sources of company news and information on the internet, as far as I'm concerned. The site has a free section and a paid subscription area that contains much more detailed information and tools. However, the free section has enough information for many investors to find all they need to know. Morningstar made its reputation providing detailed and comprehensive information on mutual funds. Later they expanded to include stocks and other securities.

Over the years, I have used both the free and paid sections. The free section has all the information you need to help you make good stock decisions. The subscription area has richer detail and comprehensive portfolio management tools. Two features stand out in my experience: the premium screen tool and the in-depth analysis. The subscription covers all of the securities Morningstar follows in addition to stocks. If you want to drill deeper, the subscription is well worth the money. However, the free resources are comprehensive and deep enough for many investors.

One of the rich features is historical data for many for the financial ratios and other metrics. This lets you see trends over long periods. How a company performs in all types of market conditions (rising or falling) and economic cycles (boom or bust) tells you what you might expect when these conditions return. An interactive chart feature lets you set different looks and compare the stock to market indexes and/or other stocks.

Yahoo! Finance

Yahoo! Finance (www.finance.yahoo.com) is a treasure chest of information on companies and stocks—along with other securities. What it lacks in design it makes up for in rich content features, including economic, market, company features, and other investing news.

One feature that stands out is their historical price database. This allows you to look back at stock prices by day or month and lets you select a date range. Using this feature, you can watch a stock's performance during the period. How did the stock's price hold up during market volatility or when there were major turns in the economy? You can download the information and open it in a program such as Microsoft Excel for further analysis.

The website reports analysts' opinions, but rather than give you the full report (some of which are available for purchase from the individual analysts), offers a summary of their findings.

For example, here is a table showing how analysts ranked one company:

Price Target	Summary
Mean target	21.71
Median target	21
High target	25
Low target	19
Number of brokers	14

At a glance, you can see that the 14 brokers that follow this stock have different opinions on the *price target* or the price they believe is appropriate for this particular stock. The consensus is around $21 per share; however, at least one felt it should be $25, while another saw it at $19. This difference of opinion is typical. At the time this information was gathered, the stock had closed the day before at $19.24 per share.

 DEFINITION

Price target is a share price analysts say the stock will achieve at some future date. Analysts often attach a period to the price, such as a one-year price target of $19. The information is more suggestive than quantifiable. It is helpful for getting a sense of what others are thinking about the stock's price.

Analysts rate companies as one of two major recommendations: "buy" or "sell," although they may use "hold" as a neutral recommendation. Some add superlatives, but another way is to use a scale that ranges from strong buy to strong sell. Here is an example from Yahoo! Finance:

Recommendation Summary*

Mean Recommendation (this week):   1.9

Mean Recommendation (last week):   1.9

Change: 0.0

*(Strong Buy) 1.0—5.0 (Sell)

This scale tells you that most analysts still feel okay about this stock, but not wildly enthusiastic, and that sentiment hasn't changed from last week.

Yahoo! Finance also has a strong charting feature, which is handy for those who prefer a visual reference to numbers. You can track stocks (or stock indexes) and compare companies in the same industry on the same chart, along with a base index.

Other Resource Websites

Following are several other websites I turn to for information, although less frequently than Morningstar or Yahoo! Finance. You may have other favorites you find helpful.

MSN.money. Microsoft Money (money.msn.com) offers many helpful tools for investing in individual stocks. In addition to comprehensive news coverage of stocks and the stock market, the site has some useful analytical tools. The feature called stockScouter ranks stocks from 1 to 10 to determine expected risk and return. You can look at individual stocks or drill down deeper into the various categories. The tool allows you to change options and effectively functions as a stock screen.

The Street. This site (thestreet.com) provides comprehensive news and information as well as several key features for stock investors. The website rates stocks using a number of factors and updates their information on a daily basis. You can look at individual stocks or an extensive list of industrial sectors. For example, they follow stocks on a watch list that may be ready to move up or down.

Forbes. Forbes is the website (forbes.com) of the venerable business magazine and has the comprehensive news coverage you would expect. It is a good resource to stay on top of company news as well as important information on changes in the economy. One of the tools you may find useful is a portfolio manager that syncs with your brokerage accounts to provide up-to-the-minute information on all of your investments. You can also enter your information manually.

Stocks About.com. Shameless self-promotion. This is a website (stocks.about.com) I write that is devoted to investing in stocks. It does not have the comprehensive financial information you'll find on the sites previously mentioned, but I do post several articles a week on investing tips and general stock information. Unlike the other websites, I am compensated for writing on this website.

Information You Should Avoid

Information on the internet ranges from incredibly useful to outright fraud. Your best bet is to stick with the websites I've previously mentioned or other mainstream sources of information. Here are some tips on information you should avoid:

- Any suggestion that you should invest in *penny stocks.*
- Any unsolicited advice you receive by email, even if it appears to be someone you know.
- Avoid any links that purport to connect you with "investor secrets revealed"; "Wall Street insider information"; "millionaire investor shares secrets"; or any other plan that promises easy riches in the stock market.
- Don't visit chat rooms or forums even on well-known websites.

There are no secrets to investing success. There is only work and a plan that fits your financial goals and tolerance for risk.

 DEFINITION

Penny stocks are a group of stocks that are not listed on any major stock exchange and trade for a few dollars a share or less. The companies are very small and have a low long-term survival rate. There is nothing wrong with most of the companies; however, penny stocks are often used in scams.

Which Numbers Are Important?

For the long-term investor, picking stocks is about understanding the important numbers. Long-term investors are not concerned with daily price fluctuations in a stock, because they are buying a company and it is the company's fundamental financial health that is important.

The value of a stock is directly related to the value of the business and is primarily concerned with earnings. The purpose of a business is to make money for its owners, and the more profitable a company is the more valuable it is to its owners and others who wish to own shares. It is easy to find historical information about a company's profits, but that is only part of the picture.

Stockholders are most interested in future profits, and historical information is not predictive of future results. A company with a lengthy history of earning consistent profits is most likely to continue that trend; however, there are no guarantees that it will.

Your job as a long-term investor is to identify companies that will meet your financial goals with an acceptable amount of risk. The selection process involves a certain amount of looking into the future and using those projections to establish the fair value for the stock today. In upcoming chapters, I help you understand how to arrive at that value using several tools in different types of analysis. I'll start with the company's financial statements, which are covered in Chapter 4.

However, before diving into the deep pool of a financial analysis, you need a way to begin the selection process by narrowing down a list of possible investment candidates to a manageable level. The best tool for this job is the stock screen.

How to Use a Stock Screen

A stock screen is a tool offered on many websites, including those mentioned in this chapter, that help investors sort through thousands of available stocks. Stock screens filter the list based on criteria you select and delivers a list of stocks that you can filter further or begin researching in depth. A good stock screen saves you time and helps you focus your research on potential investment candidates.

Stock screens range from fairly simple to quite complex. The more complex the screen, the more details it will filter for you. As you get started with screens, stick to the simpler ones and then move on to the more complicated. Many basic stock screens have presets that have already done the work of selecting the criteria for you. They can be helpful, especially when starting out in understanding how screens work; just be certain you understand what criteria the screen is using so the results are meaningful. If it helps, think of a stock screen as a search engine for stocks.

The Best Stock Screen

I use Morningstar's stock screen the most. The version on the free portion of the website is very robust and delivers excellent results. The screen in the paid area is more detailed and will take some time to master.

I like Morningstar's (free) screen for two important reasons. First, Morningstar uses some proprietary measurements on its website and on its screen. For example, they assign a grade for growth, profitability, and financial health. Morningstar also places every stock into a nine-square grid called a style box. The style box uses growth, core, and value across the top and large, mid, or small along the side. This puts every stock into a square based on its size and type.

All of the proprietary measurements, along with traditional metrics, are defined throughout the site. For example, in the stock screen, each criterion has a light bulb icon next to its name. When you click on the light bulb, a window opens with the definition or explanation of the variable.

STOCK TIP

The task of mastering the stock screen tool is the most important objective in the early stages of learning about investing in stocks. Whether you use Morningstar's or another, a good knowledge of the stock screen is vital to your success.

Using Morningstar's Stock Screen

The first tab on Morningstar's screen is where you set the criteria for the search. On your first use of the screen, you may encounter some terms you don't understand, although they are all explained in the "light bulb" windows. Don't worry about the terms you don't understand, I'll cover these and more in Chapters 6 and 7.

The best way to use a screen is to start with just a few criteria selected to begin building a list for further refinement. The screen will work with just a few of the variables selected, although you will get a large list. After you've made your first selection, you can view the results, then go back, and add in additional variables. Your initial selections are saved until you start a new screen.

For example, if I select Large Core, minimum market capitalization of $10 billion, and a profitability grade of "A," the Morningstar screen currently returns 15 results. That's a great start, but 15 stocks are still too many to research in depth.

The screen allows me to go back to the criteria page and add or change my selections. If I go to the Financial Health choice and click A and B, the screen will look for the same stocks as before, but with a Financial Health grade of A or B. Now I am down to nine stocks. If I ask for a Five-Year Forecasted Earnings Growth of greater than or equal to 10 percent, the screen narrows the field down to two stocks.

As you become more familiar with the terms used in the stock screen, you will be able to select more criteria on the first search and narrow your results faster. It's important to have a working knowledge of the various numbers and ratios to fully use and understand the screen—all of which are covered in this book.

Financial Statements

If the thought of analyzing financial statements intimidates you, welcome to the crowd. People spend years in college learning to analyze financial statements, and this book will not replicate those years of study. However, you will come away with a better understanding of what the numbers mean and which ones are really important to your analysis.

Financial statements contain the history of what happened to the company during a certain period. The law requires that publicly traded companies provide audited financial statements that are available for review. Accounting firms verify that the numbers are correct and sign the audit.

Although it is certainly possible to play fast and loose with the numbers, investors can be confident that for the most part what they are seeing is an accurate description of the company's finances. It's important to note that all financial statements are historical in nature, which means they reflect what has happened in the recent past, but say nothing about what may happen in the future.

In upcoming chapters, I will cover several ways to place a value on a company, that is, a fair price for its stock. These valuation processes use numbers from the financial statements to generate their conclusions. It is important that investors have an idea about where the numbers come from, why they are significant, and where there are flaws in the reporting.

Company Reports (Financially) Tell All

Publically traded companies must provide detailed reports to investors and the Securities Exchange Commission (SEC). These documents contain the three financial statements I discuss in this chapter. The most familiar of these documents is the annual report, which companies are required to file at the end of their fiscal year. Most companies have a fiscal year that coincides with the calendar year; however, some start their fiscal year in months other than January. Apple, Inc., for example, has a *fiscal year* that ends on September 24.

 DEFINITION

> **Fiscal year** is a way to define the period covered by a company's financial statements. Most companies use a fiscal year that begins January 1 and ends December 31. Others choose different dates for their fiscal year. For example, Apple's 2013 fiscal year begins September 30, 2012.

The annual report is usually printed in a magazine format with photographs of happy customers and grateful employees. The real meat of the report is not found until near the end when the three financial statements are presented along with the accountant's certification of accuracy. Some companies will mail you an annual report and you can often find the details on the company's website under investor relations.

The 10-K is another version of the annual report, but this is a document the company is required to file with the SEC. It is all business and none of the glossy pictures and glowing text that is often found in the annual report. The 10-K has more information and goes into greater detail, including reports on risks the company faces, than the annual report and you can get it for free by going to the SEC website where you can download the report or from the investor relations section of the company's website.

The 10-Q is also required by the SEC, but is filed on a quarterly basis. These can be very helpful because they provide more current information than the annual report or the 10-K. The 10-Q is also available for download from the SEC and from some companies' websites. Most 10-Q reports are unaudited.

Three Main Financial Statements

There are three main financial statements that you will use when analyzing a company. From the statements, you can draw conclusions about the relative health of the company and make some guesses about its financial future. You will find the financial statements in the documents previously discussed.

The three financial statements I cover include ...

- The balance sheet
- The income statement
- The statement of cash flows

Together these three reports give you enough information to perform a valuation of the business. The three financial statements give you three different views of the company's performance, but they all tie together to make a complete picture.

The Balance Sheet Must Balance

The balance sheet, also known as the statement of financial position, is a snapshot of the company's financial strength at the end of the fiscal year. The statement details what the company owns and what it owes. It does not show money flowing in or out (that's on the statement of cash flows), but gives you a snapshot of whether this is a viable business or not.

It is called a balance sheet because it must balance. The balance is often expressed as this formula:

assets = liabilities + (shareholders) equity

or

(shareholders) equity = assets − liabilities

The three terms that make up the formula are the heart of what the balance sheet tells you about the company.

Assets: What the Company Owns

Assets represent what the company owns. The expectation is that assets are something that can provide economic value to the company. This can be as straightforward as buildings, real estate, and equipment and materials used for production. Obviously, cash and investments represent assets the company can use.

However, there are other categories of assets that are not so tangible. For example, if a company buys another company, it usually pays more than the actual cash value. The difference is called goodwill and represents the value of the acquired company beyond its cash value. For example, if you wanted to buy Apple, Inc., you would pay much more than the buildings, equipment, and so on is worth. The Apple name and brand would be worth many times the tangible assets it processes.

Assets are also broken down by whether the company plans to use them in one year—called current assets. These include cash, inventory (in most cases), short-term investments, and accounts receivable. Accounts receivable represent money the company expects to collect from customers but has not received. Accounts receivable is a particularly important number. Companies use accrual accounting that allows them to book a sale, even if the customer hasn't paid the bill, as long as there is a reasonable expectation of payment. This number shows up on the income statement as revenue, even though no money has changed hands. It is counted on the balance sheet as an asset because the customer is expected to pay this fiscal year.

STOCK TIP

Companies have their own special way of accounting for certain transactions. One of the most confusing allows a company to book a sale as revenue even if the client hasn't paid. This is an important point to remember when looking at the balance sheet and income statement; however, it does not apply to the statement of cash flows.

Noncurrent assets include property, buildings, and equipment, which represent an economic value, but are not expected to be converted to cash. Other assets, another noncurrent asset, may include items such as intellectual properties or other items that may be peculiar to that industry. For example, a bank's balance sheet would feature some different items than a manufacturing company.

Unfortunately, there is not a standard nomenclature for balance sheets, so you may see different categories represented on some statements. However, the idea is to capture all that the company owns that is of economic value. The total of all these items is the company's total assets.

Liabilities: What the Company Owes

What a company owes are its liabilities. Like assets, liabilities are divided into current and noncurrent. Current liabilities are those bills that must be paid within one year, some obviously sooner. These include bills for materials, parts, or other obligations.

Most of these fall into the accounts payable category. This is an important number because it represents money that must be paid out quickly. Does the company have the resources to meet these obligations? A reading of current assets will give you a good idea.

Companies have other operating expenses, including the cost of running the business on a daily basis: payroll, current taxes, utilities, and so on. All of these represent drains on cash, which can be a concern if the company has trouble collecting the accounts receivable. Because of the drain on cash of current liabilities, companies often use short-term borrowing to cover the gap. These are current liabilities and if the company has huge amounts of short-term borrowing, it may mean trouble.

Noncurrent liabilities represent long-term debt, such as paying off bonds it has issued in the past or long-term financing of plants and equipment. Long-term debt is an important number because it represents a continuing drain on the company's cash. Some types of businesses require more debt than others. For example, manufacturers may need to borrow hundreds of millions of dollars to build new plants and buy new equipment. Service-related companies, such as software companies, may not need that level of long-term debt.

Shareholders Equity: Value to Investors

Shareholders or stockholders equity is value in the company that is owned by shareholders. Remember the formula:

(shareholders) equity = assets − liabilities

A home mortgage is a simple example: the equity in your home is the difference between the fair market value (assets) − the balance of your mortgage (liabilities) = your equity. Unfortunately, if you owe more than your house is worth, you have a negative equity. A company faces the same reality. If it loses money, the stockholder's equity could be negative or reduced from the previous year.

A company's shareholder's equity section on the balance sheet may have several entries, but the most important one is retained earnings. This entry represents the beginning capital that financed the company's start and any earnings that are not paid out in dividends. Some companies pay no dividends, so their retained earnings entry will grow from year to year, as long as they are making a profit. However, most companies use retained earnings to pay off long-term debt, buy new equipment, or otherwise reinvest in the company. Paying for these items out of retained earnings means the company does not have to borrow more money.

MARKET RISK

When reviewing financial statements, be aware that the term "income" doesn't mean the money coming into the company. Income loosely means profit, although there are several types of income.

The Income Statement Is Home to Bottom Line

While many investors and the media focus on the income statement (this is where you find the magic "bottom line"), it only provides part of the picture for any business. Still, the income statement reports whether the business made or lost money. It is easy for some to confuse the income statement with their checkbook. Did I take in more than I spent, and if so, did I make a "profit" this month?

As you might suspect, it is a little more complicated than that. The ability to record a sale before the company is paid is only one of the complicating factors that haunt the income statement.

The income statement has three major sections:

- Revenue
- Expenses
- Earnings or Income

Look at any income statement and you will quickly notice that it reports more than one type of profit or income.

Revenue Is Sales

Revenue, or as it is sometimes called, sales, represents the money resulting from the company's business operations. The income statement may add subcategories based on product lines, countries, or other factors. The 10-K usually labels these revenues as consolidated, meaning the company lumped several businesses or business units into one statement.

The next major item on most income statements is an expense called cost of goods sold (COGS). This item lists the direct expenses that are tied to producing goods or services for sales. For example, labor costs, cost of raw materials, and cost of inventory bought for resale or used in manufacturing. Sales expenses, distribution costs, and other expenses not directly related to producing the product or service are excluded from COGS. When you subtract COGS from the sales number, you get gross profit. Although it is not on the income statement, you can calculate an important metric called gross margin. Gross margin is the gross profit as a percentage of revenues. The gross margin lets you compare one company to another in the same business. If a company has a higher gross margin than its competitors, then it is more efficient at making its goods and may have an advantage in the market, because it could lower its price and perhaps capture a larger share of its market from its competitors.

Expenses: The Cost of Doing Business

Next on the income statement are the expenses associated with operating the business. These include selling expenses, administrative expenses, marketing, and research and development. Depending on the business, some items such as research and development or advertising (marketing) may be reported on a separate line. Other expenses are often listed separately. You can find more information on all items in the income statement in the company's 10-K. If the company made money on some non-business-related transaction, it is recorded here and noted in parentheses, because this is an expense area.

Also lumped in operating expenses are items such as depreciation, one-time charges, and gains. If the company closes a plant, the costs associated with that do not represent ongoing expenses, but must be recorded as a charge against earnings. Likewise, the profit from a sale of a product line is a one-time event and is recorded as a negative expense. When you deduct operating expenses from the gross profit, you come up with operating income.

Operating Income: Sales Minus Cost of Sales

In its pure form, operating income should be the company's revenue minus the cost of goods sold and minus the operating expenses. This number tells you how much the company made on its business operations and is the most important number when analyzing the company. However, as I noted previously, companies can stuff nonrecurring and other one-time expenses into the operating expenses, so you need to deduct those from the operating expenses totals to get a true operating income number. Many financial websites make this calculation for you.

Net Income: The Bottom Line

The net income is what most consider the bottom line; however, before you get to that number, there are deductions for taxes, interest expenses, and (income) and other one-time expenses or investment income. Yet, this is the number most reported by the company and the media. The net income figure is divided by outstanding shares to arrive at the earnings per share (EPS) number. In Chapter 6, I show you how this metric is used and widely misused.

When you analyze a company, the operating income is more important than the net income because it gives you a picture of how healthy the business is, especially compared to its peers.

STOCK TIP

You seldom hear the media report off of the statement of cash flows, but it contains some of the most important information you need to analyze a company for possible investment.

Statement of Cash Flows Tracks Cash In and Out

The statement of cash flows is the most important of the three financial statements, because it deals with how much cash came into the business and how much went out. The difference is cash left for reinvestment, dividends, and so on. How much cash a company generates after expenses is ultimately why you buy its stock. Companies that have a large and growing positive cash flow (more in than out) generate value for the shareholders. A company's future cash flows (projections) help analysts set a value for the stock today, because a company is worth the discounted value of future cash flows. I discuss this in more detail in Chapter 6, but for now it is important to understand where those numbers come from and why they are important.

The statement of cash flows is broken into three parts: cash flows from operations, investing activities, and financing activities. The important thing to remember about the statement of cash flows is that it does not contain nuances, noncash expenses, or other vague accounting actions.

Cash Flows from Operating Activities

This part of the statement starts with net income, which comes right off the income statement. However, remember that the net income figure included charges for noncash items such as depreciation, which has to be added back in to the statement. Other charges and expenses are adjusted as they affect cash. For example, a pension obligation is deducted from net income because it represents cash leaving the business. Changes in inventory also cause adjustments, because a higher level of inventory than the previous year takes cash out of the business.

You will notice that the statement of cash flows often lists one or more previous years. This is where changes in inventory, accounts payable, accounts receivables, and so on are reconciled. The change in inventory previously mentioned is seen in the side-by-side listings for the current and previous years. The numbers come from the balance sheet or, in some cases, the income statement. What you are looking for is how those changes affect the cash flowing through the company. Higher accounts receivable than the previous year means less cash is available, while higher accounts payable (bills the company owes, but has not paid) from the previous year means more cash stays in the company. Depending on the type of business, there will be other additions and subtractions from the net income figure. The final adjustment is accounting for any one-time, noncash charges that were on the income statement. These could be related to an acquisition or other charges. All of these are found on the income statement and should be added back in to the net income.

After all these adjustments, the statement of cash flows produces the net cash from operating activities. This number tells you how much cash the business is generating and is known as operating cash flow. This is the most important figure on all three financial statements. If a company has a strong and growing operating cash flow, it is probably a serious candidate for investment. Obviously, if the opposite is the case, you may want to walk away without too much more research.

Cash Flows from Financing Activities

Dividends are found in this section, if the company pays dividends. Dividends are a way the company returns some of the profits to shareholders. While they represent a charge against cash, dividends are a good thing and many investors look for companies that pay consistent and growing dividends. The other changes in cash in this section have to do with issuing or repurchasing stock (not every company will have these every year), issuing or repaying long-term debt, and other financing charges. Remember, this statement is about cash in and cash out, so if a company issues bonds, which are long-term debt, the proceeds are added to cash.

What the Statement of Cash Flows Tells You

After all the adjustments (adding in or subtracting out), the statement of cash flows tells you whether the company took more in than it paid out for the year and, when compared to previous years, whether cash flows is growing or shrinking. In most cases, you will want to see cash flows growing from year to year, but there may be good reasons for it not to if the company is investing heavily in its growth (new buildings, equipment, and so on). The statement of cash flows pulls together the balance sheet, which is a static, one-day snapshot of the company and the income statement, which features many noncash expenses and other nonoperating costs and revenue.

Your goal is a company with strong core operations that is generating lots of cash after investing in its own growth. The statement of cash flows tells you this information without any of the fuzzy noncash, one-time charges found elsewhere.

Types of Stocks

Stocks can be divided into categories or classes. While you may think in terms of a "technology stock" or a "health care stock," this is just one of many ways to categorize stocks. Another way to organize stocks is by the main reason investors are interested in individual stocks—their attributes in the market. This method is one of the most basic and remains one of the most important methods of organizing stocks.

What is gained by organizing stocks? For one thing, organized stocks can be compared with other stocks in the same category. This is helpful in understanding whether a stock is outside the norm for its category. In this chapter, I look at the most basic categories: growth, value, and core stocks. I also explain why a company's size (based on its value in the stock market) is an important way to compare stocks. Then I discuss economic sectors and how they play a role in stock selection.

Growth Stocks

Growth stocks are those that take off and never seem to retreat in price—at least that's what investors hope. In truth, no stock rises in a straight line forever—sometimes not even for very long. Even true growth stocks have periods when the price falls back, but the growth pattern resumes eventually or they cease to be growth stocks. Growth stocks rise faster than the market in general in price and earnings. Technology stocks, for example, are often labeled growth stocks.

By their very nature, growth stocks can be exciting and glamorous. The hype surrounding a hot stock can be seductive, but you will almost always be buying at a premium price, which can make it difficult or impossible to turn a profit. The trick is to know what price the stock is worth.

Defining "Growth"

Growth stocks should grow faster than the overall market. In down or declining markets, this may mean they don't fall as far or as fast as the rest of the market.

Growth rates usually differ between smaller and larger companies. It is difficult to maintain a rapid growth for larger companies, while young companies may post impressive growth rates, in part, because they start from a relatively low base. It is much easier to double a $10 million dollar company than it is to double a $10 billion company.

Another important characteristic of a growth stock is that they seldom pay dividends. Growth companies usually require considerable capital to fund the expansion companies and are more likely to reinvest profits (if any) to pay for more growth than pay dividends. Finally, an important characteristic of many growth stocks is that they're overpriced. Growth stocks often command premium prices, which makes it difficult to make money unless you know at what price to buy.

STOCK TIP

The two most important prices you need to focus on getting right are the price when you buy and the price when you sell. Otherwise, don't sweat daily price fluctuations unless you are ready to buy or sell.

Growth Stock Characteristics

Another common feature of growth stocks is size. In general, a smaller company is more likely to have a growth stock than a larger company. That is not a hard-and-fast rule because some large companies have growth stocks, but it is a good way to begin understanding growth stocks in general. Here are some more important characteristics of growth stocks:

Growth stocks can be volatile. Because investors fall in and out of love frequently with growth companies, their stock prices often bounce up and down, sometimes with breathtaking drama. Growth stocks that disappoint investors by not growing or not growing enough are often dumped quickly, leading to stock price drops.

Growth is not just about stock price. Growth companies post rising numbers in several key indicators. Investors expect rising revenues, rising profits, and a rising stock price. In addition, investors want to see a company post solid returns, such as return on equity and other key measures. However, some young growth companies may go for several years with no earnings (profits) due to the cost of rapid expansion. Many run out of money before ever making a profit.

Growth over peers. Investors want to see the company posting growth rates that match or exceed peers and competitors. By classifying stocks, we can compare them with industry peers and the market in general. A growth company that consistently posts numbers below its peers or competitors would need other compelling reasons to attract many investors.

Risk. Growth stocks are generally more risky than other types of stocks. The reasons include slowing growth rates, falling out of favor with investors, advances in technology, or other factors that threaten the company's economic market position. Smaller companies are often targets of takeovers by larger competitors anxious to grab market share (takeovers can be good for smaller companies, in some cases, because bidding often boosts stock prices). The brutal reality of the economy and the stock market is that many small companies will fail. However, those that survive have an opportunity to grow into industry leaders.

Taking a Chance on Growth Stocks

Investing in the stock market is about the future, and growth stocks often hold the promise of better than average returns in the future. Unfortunately, that promise of greater returns is often unfulfilled as rising stock market stars slip and fall. One of the most important pieces of making growth stocks work for you is understanding when (at what price) to buy and, equally important, when to sell.

At times the stock market goes crazy over some sector of the economy that seems to be booming, such as the tech sector in the late 1990s. The same thing happened in 2008 when the financial crisis caused by the housing market collapse and the popping of the bubble in worthless mortgage-backed securities destroyed trillions of dollars in value out of the stock market. At the beginning of 2000, Apple Inc. was trading at $100 per share, but by April of 2012 the per-share price was more than $600. Considering that during the intervening years, there were two recessions, the 9/11 attacks, and a financial crisis that crippled the U.S. economy, the stock's growth has been phenomenal.

Your challenge, if you want to invest in small growth companies, is to identify companies that have a reasonably good chance of gaining market share and growing without being taken over by a larger competitor or losing a technology or marketing race.

However, remember Apple and Microsoft were both once very small companies with an idea.

MARKET RISK

The definition of a "hot" market for many savvy investors is a time to consider selling and taking profits. Unfortunately, too many investors decide that is the time to begin investing.

Value Stocks

The second major definition of stocks is called value stock. Value stocks represent the unappreciated and underappreciated stocks on the market. The companies behind value stocks have good financial health and may be doing relatively well in their markets, but for some reason the stock market does not appreciate the stock's potential. When tech stocks are all the rage, growth investors want tech stocks and not metal fabricators or service or retail stocks. Because they are not in a hot industry sector, value stocks often languish until the market re-discovers their potential.

As unglamorous as value stocks may seem, many investors have done very well carefully looking for those companies trading significantly below their true value. Because most value stocks do not attract attention, there is a good chance you can buy them at reasonable prices. It is rumored that Warren Buffett, the most successful investor in the United States, made investing in value stocks the basis of his investment philosophy.

Not Cheap Stocks

Value stocks are not "cheap" stocks, which indicates their prices are low or the stocks are nearly worthless. The feature that identifies a value stock is the price relationship to the company's real value, as determined by the investor. The share price is only a factor as it relates to other stocks.

The very small companies may or may not be bargains. You can't tell by the share price of any stock whether it is a bargain or overpriced. That determination takes more examination.

Value Stock Characteristics

Value investors look for stocks with certain characteristics. There is no universally accepted definition of value stocks, so you may see other characteristics identified than the ones listed here. The point is to develop a profile of a value stock, so you can judge stocks on the same basis. Some of the terms may be new to you, but don't worry, I'll cover them in more detail in Chapter 7. And you shouldn't stress over any math involved in these numbers, they are all readily available on the internet:

- The price earnings ratio (P/E) should be in the bottom 10 percent of all companies.

- A price to earning growth ratio (PEG) should be less than 1, which indicates the company is undervalued.

- There should be at least as much equity as debt.

- Current assets should be twice the current liabilities.

- Share price should be at tangible book value or less.

- The stocks should frequently have a high dividend yield.

STOCK TIP

Don't worry about memorizing all the basic numbers. Just get a general sense of what they mean and how to use them. The actual numbers are available for all companies for free on many financial websites, such as Morningstar.com or Yahoo! Finance.

When you have some experience with stocks, you may want to add to or subtract from this list. For example, some value investors want to see the stock hit a 52-week low as part of their screening.

The Value Stock Investor

As with value stocks, the value stock investor exhibits certain characteristics in the way they buy and sell. Hard-core value investors stick to a rigid investment strategy. Most investors lack the time to focus as intently on just value stocks. In addition, many investors will mix their investment strategies, including growth and other stocks along with their value investments. Here are some of the characteristics of a value investor:

Loves the businesses he buys. Value investors tend to be passionate about the companies they invest in, wanting to know all the details about the company, including financials, market strategy, and more. While this passion can be helpful in motivating the value investor, be careful that it doesn't blind you to shortcomings or warning signs.

Understands the businesses she buys. The value investor does her homework. She can explain what the company does (how it makes money), what its market is, and what companies are competitors. You should know enough to see how it fits into the economy and where it is strong and where it is vulnerable.

Looks for great management. Great companies have great managers. Great managers make decisions more like owners than caretakers. Often strategic decisions that help the company in the long run impact short-term numbers. Owners do what is best for the company's long-term future.

Frequently reviews their decisions. Value investors often don't own a large number of stocks, because analyzing the businesses and frequently reviewing for any changes is time-consuming.

Long-Term Buy

Value stocks are long-term buys, which fit nicely into most investors' plans. If you have picked a great company with a stock that is languishing, be willing to hold the stock until other investors discover the same thing. As with all your stock buys, check on the company quarterly to make sure it is still the great company you bought.

Value stocks, even when other investors discover them, tend to rise over time, rather than shoot through the roof. A benefit of owning some value stocks is they often pay dividends. This income may make it easier to hold a stock that is not climbing in price.

Core Stocks

As you might guess from the name, core stocks are the foundation for your investment plan. It would be easy to assume that core stocks fall somewhere between growth and value stocks, but that isn't quite right. While they do grow at a fairly reliable rate, they are seldom growth superstars. Because they are popular foundation buys, not only for individuals but also institutional investors, mutual funds and other big investors, they tend to be fairly priced over time. You will seldom find a core stock dramatically underpriced the way value stocks are.

Core stocks are always large companies and could rightly be called "blue chip" stocks. Think of the 30 stocks that make up the Dow. However, there are plenty of stocks that fit the qualifications for core stocks beyond those in the Dow. Conservative investors may have all or much of their portfolio in core stocks, which is not a bad strategy.

Core Stock Characteristics

Mutual funds and other institutional investors have guidelines for buying core stocks, and you should, too. To help you form your own guidelines for investing in core stocks, here are some of the key characteristics:

Core stocks represent big companies. Large companies tend to be older with mature markets. Size is usually an advantage in competitive markets. While they may not be as nimble as smaller competitors, core companies have financial, marketing, and other assets that help them weather difficult economies and market changes.

Core stocks make money. Core stock investors look for companies that are profitable year after year. In addition to regular profits (earnings), great core companies are good investments when bought at the right price. It is this consistent return and the stability of it that earn core stocks their high regard in the investment community.

STOCK TIP

Core stocks should make money; that is profitable. A large company does not necessarily make a good investment or a core stock. Do your homework to find true core stocks.

Core stocks grow. Despite their size, core stocks manage to consistently post growth in revenue and earnings. Core stocks will seldom jump dramatically as smaller companies often do. However, they can be counted on to grow earnings, which usually lead to higher stock prices. Core stocks often pay dividends, which add to investors' returns with annual income.

Core stocks have strong financials. Core stocks tend to have very strong financial statements that reflect little debt, strong cash flow, and other key metrics covered in Chapter 4. They are not going out of business anytime soon.

Safety and Stability

Not all large companies qualify as core stocks because of toxic financial statements, out-of-date products and services, and many other reasons. Look at all of the previously listed characteristics and add some of your own when you become more familiar with investing in stocks.

True core stocks provide a measure of safety and stability to your portfolio. That doesn't mean they are completely safe investments that you don't need to monitor. The stock market graveyard is littered with large companies that failed to protect their market share or lost track of their customers' needs.

The Cost of Safety

Core stocks are attractive to many investors from individuals to institutional investors, which means you will not find them on sale frequently. When the stock market is declining or the economy shaky, there is often a "flight to safety," which includes core stocks (also bonds and cash). The movement of capital to core stocks from other investments tends to push up the price. Even when the stock market is excited about a sector or group of stocks, core stocks hold up well in price because conservative investors will not sell just to chase the latest fad.

Size Matters in Stocks

One of the ways you analyze stocks is to compare key metrics to other stocks of the same size and industry sector. I discuss industrial sectors in the next section of this chapter. Company size is important for two reasons:

- *Companies of different sizes behave differently.* A company with sales in the tens of billions of dollars and with thousands of employees will not respond to market conditions the same way as a company with 100 employees and a couple of million dollars in sales. If you want to know if the large company is performing well, you compare it to companies of roughly the same size.

- *Large companies are less risky.* Small companies have a high mortality rate, which makes them more risky than large companies. The more risk you take, the larger the potential reward must be. Larger companies are less risky and do not command a risk premium.

A large company is no guarantee of safety for investors, nor is a small company doomed to failure. However, if you want to minimize risk, stick with larger companies. There are several ways to define the size of a business, such as annual revenue, number of employees, and so on. The standard way of defining size is market cap.

MARKET RISK

Sales or revenue is not a good way to classify stocks. Some companies can generate tremendous sales, but fail to make a profit, while other companies may have modest sales, but post big profits. Which do you want to own?

Market cap, shorthand for market capitalization, is a way of defining the size of companies. It is simply the number of outstanding (available shares held by the public) shares of common stock times the stock's per-share price. For example, a company with one million shares of outstanding stock and a per-share price of $10 would have a market cap of $10 million.

Here is how I, and many other financial professionals, define the market cap ranges:

- Mega-cap stocks—market cap in excess of $200 billion
- Large-cap stocks—market cap from $10 billion to $200 billion
- Mid-cap stocks—market cap from $2 billion to $10 billion
- Small-cap stocks—market cap from $300 million to $2 billion

As you can see, there are some wide ranges in the rankings. For example, large-cap stocks range from $10 billion to $200 billion. That range covers a wide variety of sizes. Here's where stock screens can come in handy. Depending on the screen, you can usually narrow the ranges so you are getting a closer comparison than the general market cap rankings provide. This gives you a better idea of how the company compares to others that are close to its size.

Stock Sectors

One of the ways investors classify stocks is by type of business. The idea is to put companies in similar industries together for comparison purposes. These groupings are called "sectors" and you will often read or hear about how certain stock sectors are performing ("Tech stocks up today," for example).

One of the most common classifications breaks the market into 11 different sectors; however, you may see other sector lists that have more than 11. It's not particularly important which list you choose, but stick to one to keep comparisons valid. I like the 11-sector list for its simplicity.

Investors consider two of the sectors "defensive" and the remaining nine "cyclical." Let's look at these two categories and see what they mean for the individual investor.

Defensive Sectors Defined

Defensive sectors, also known as noncyclical, include utilities and consumer staples (think energy, food, and toilet paper, for example). These companies usually don't suffer as much in a market downturn because people don't stop using energy or eating. They provide a balance to portfolios and offer protection in a falling market.

However, for all their safety, defensive stocks usually fail to climb with a rising market for the opposite reasons they provide protection in a falling market: people don't use significantly more energy or eat more food.

Defensive stocks do exactly what their name implies, assuming they are well-run companies. They give you a cushion for a soft landing in a falling market. For conservative investors, they offer a relatively stable anchor amid market chaos. Defensive stocks also pay dividends and should be considered as part of your core investments.

STOCK TIP

Conservative investors favor portfolios with more defensive stocks. This is a fine strategy, but not one that will serve young investors, who should be more focused on growing their portfolio.

Cyclical Sectors Defined

Cyclical stocks, on the other hand, cover everything else and tend to react to a variety of market conditions that can send them up or down. However, when one sector is going up another may be going down.

Here is a list of the nine sectors considered cyclical:

Basic materials. Basic materials include those items used in making other goods—lumber, for instance. When the housing market is active, the stock of lumber companies tends to rise.

Capital goods. The capital goods sector contains manufacturers of industrial equipment, defense (as in military) goods, aerospace, construction, and so on. This sector is also very sensitive to the economy.

Communications. These companies are in the telecommunications business as well as wireless (cell phones, for example) carriers.

Consumer cyclical. This sector is very sensitive to the economy. It includes automotive, entertainment, retail, and housing. When the economy is good, these sectors flourish. Not so much in a slow economy.

Energy. This sector includes those companies involved in the exploration for and distribution of natural resources such as coal, oil, gas, and so on, but not utilities.

Financial. The companies in this sector include banks and other deposit-taking companies such as stock market participants (brokers, investment banks, and so on).

Health care. The health care sector includes hospitals, clinics, health care management companies, and medical products. Some put this sector in the defensive category because people still need care. However, in tough economic times, people will put off preventative care, for example.

Technology. This sector contains companies that make their money on their technology or supplying technology companies.

Computer manufacturers, software, hardware, and so on are some of the products they produce. New or significant advances in technology can cause a stir and push this sector up.

Transportation. Airlines, trucking companies, railroads, and other companies that move goods or people make up this sector.

Companies in the various sectors may or may not react the same as the whole sector, which can indicate good or poor management depending on the way the company moves.

Stock Price vs. Stock Value

How much is a share of stock worth? This is the fundamental question you must answer to successfully invest in stocks. If you don't know what a share is worth, how will you know if you're paying too much or getting a great bargain? The daily price on the stock market is often not much help. Long-term investors are focused on buying great companies that will deliver value for years to come. Finding great companies is only half the problem. The other half is buying the stock at a price that offers plenty of room for growth. The stock's daily price in the stock market is determined by many factors other than just the value of the company. Arriving at the value of the company means considering both the tangible and intangible assets, how well the company protects itself from competitors, and how fundamentally sound its financial statements are.

No Clear Answers on Stock Prices

Determining a stock's price is more complicated than it may appear. In reality, a stock has several prices all set in different ways by different participants in the stock market. How these prices and participants interact is what makes the stock market an interesting and challenging puzzle to solve. Contrary to some perceptions, there is no smoke-filled room where stock market kingpins sit around a table and set prices. Daily prices on the stock market are, for the most part, totally uncontrolled and likely to do almost anything. The price the stock market reports is just one price of several that investors must deal with. Long-term investors analyze businesses in an attempt to find a fair market value. This number can be very different from the daily stock price. Which price is correct? They both are, actually.

How do you figure a price that represents what the company is truly worth? There are several processes, and most investors use more than one. It would be nice if you could plug in some numbers to a formula and come up with an answer, but it is not that simple. Putting a value on a business and thus its stock is part science and part art. If it were not so, everyone would have the same number; however, a quick look at Morningstar.com or Finance.Yahoo.com will reveal a wide range of opinions on most stocks by various analysts.

 MARKET RISK

Beware of advice or a tip that a certain stock is going to double (or more) in price very soon and now is the time to go all in to make a killing. The advice is either ignorance or, more likely, the front end of a scheme to take your money. Anyone who "knows" a stock is going to double in price is either illegally trading with insider information or a fraud.

How Daily Stock Prices Are Set

Stock prices change every time shares are bought and sold. For stocks that are heavily traded, the price can change several times a second and many hundreds of times during the trading day. What causes the price of stocks to rise and fall during the trading day? The media report that stock prices were up or down for some particular news event. Whether it is rising inflation or unrest in the Middle East, media pundits want a quick and simple answer to why the market was up or down on a particular day.

Economic news, global news, and other events do affect stock market prices. However, these events are just the catalyst for more basic actions and reactions that are the true drivers of daily stock market prices. The simple but powerful forces of supply and demand set stock prices on a daily basis. If there are more buyers in the market for a stock than sellers, the price will go up as buyers raise their offers to entice stockholders to sell. If there are more sellers in the market for stock than buyers, the price goes down as sellers lower the price they will take to attract buyers.

Ultimately, the price of the stock is equal to what a willing buyer and a willing seller agree upon. However, in the heat of daily stock trading this price may or may not be close to the fair market value. Your job as an investor is to determine the fair market value of the stock and compare that to its daily price on the stock market. This comparison tells you whether it is a good time to buy (or sell) the stock or not.

Price and Value Are Not the Same

Don't confuse price and value when investing in the stock market. A stock's price in daily trading can be pushed and pulled by many influences. However, the value of the business is not changed by fluctuations in the stock's price. The value you determine in your analysis establishes the fair market value of the stock, at least as far as you are concerned. This fair market value is also called its intrinsic value, which means it reflects the value of the business to investors.

Intrinsic Value Determines Potential Success

Investors who guess at a stock's fair market value will soon find themselves wondering where all their money went, because they will not know if they are paying too much for the stock. Smart investors buy a business, not a stock. They analyze the business using proven formulas and arrive at a price for the stock that reflects the value to investors. That price is the stock's intrinsic value, which considers all of the company's assets, both tangible and intangible. When you know the intrinsic value of a company, you can decide whether the stock is overpriced, underpriced, or priced about where it should be. All investors should avoid over-paying for a stock. If this seems like obvious common sense, you are right, but it is not an approach all investors follow.

Some investors tell themselves all sorts of stories to justify pay-ing more for a stock than its intrinsic value. However, smart investors are patient and wait for a stock that can be bought at a price that gives them a reasonable chance of making a profit. That patience is one of the distinguishing features of a long-term investor. Buying great companies at a great price is the recipe for success.

The process of determining the intrinsic value of a stock involves two broad steps. There is no particular order to the steps. If you encounter major problems with either step, you may want to skip straight to another investment candidate. The two steps are shown here:

1. Determine a price for the stock that reflects its value to investors.

2. Determine if the company has a sustainable economic advantage or moat.

Of the two, analyzing the company's *economic moat* is a bit more subjective. However, if the company has no economic moat or one that appears unsustainable, I would suggest you pass on that stock and move on to another.

DEFINITION

The terms **economic moat** and competitive advantage mean roughly the same thing. Other synonyms exist, but essentially the economic moat represents those qualities that make the company a leader in its field and in a place that is easy to defend.

Analyzing a Company's Economic Moat

An economic moat protects a company from being over-run by competitors. It is not a guarantee against competitors capturing market share, but its strength can slow them down. A strong economic moat today does not mean it will last forever. In the early days of computers, IBM had a lock on most of the business. While it is still a strong company, the industry has evolved and is full of competitors. Great companies adapt to changes in technology and the market.

An economic moat is important in determining the company's intrinsic value, because it gives you some idea of the potential long-term success of the company. As a long-term investor, you are looking for companies that can deliver value to stockholders for years to come. A strong economic moat is part of the answer to that question. Determining how a strong economic moat protects a company begins with a look at its financial health. The best way to find this information is to visit one of the websites discussed in Chapter 3, such as Morningstar, and find the following suggested indicators. The next step in analyzing a company's economic moat is evaluating how deep and wide it is.

Strong History of Making Money

It is not enough for a company to be profitable today—you should be interested in companies that have been making money for years. Has the company been profitable in good economies and bad? Has the company grown revenue and earnings? Does the company generate a strong free cash stream? These are all signs of a company that is at the top of its market. Morningstar shows you five years on its free side and ten years on the subscription side. Ten years would be better, but five years will do.

Financial ratios are tools investors use to measure the health of a company. They are also good ways to compare one company to another and you can compare a company to its industry sector. Most ratios have some flaws, so you should never rely on a single metric.

Here are some markers of profitability:

Earnings growth. Look for companies that post year-to-year growth in earnings (an occasional hiccup during recessions is acceptable). Although this is not a perfect metric (remember accounting charges can reduce earnings), it is one you should look at. Make sure the target company is reporting earnings substantially higher than its sector (you can find these numbers in Yahoo! Finance in the stock research section). Also, compare it to major competitors.

Free cash flow. Great companies generate a lot of cash and, particularly, have a large flow of free cash. Free cash is what is left over after the company reinvests in itself to keep the business operating. Another way to think of this is how much cash you could pull out of the business without forcing a change in operations (closing plants, layoffs, and so on).

Return on assets (ROA). How efficient is the company in generating earnings? Great companies have a superior return on assets to their sector. This measure tells investors the company is using assets wisely and creating value for the owners. For example, two companies each have $100 in assets. One company uses those assets to create $5 in earnings, while the other company uses the same amount of assets to create $15 in earnings. Which would you choose to own? Compare companies in the same sector for a valid check.

Return on equity (ROE). Another way to look at a company's profit-generating efficiency figures in how the company uses debt in addition to assets. Because most companies use some debt to run the business, it is important to take it into consideration. ROE considers how well the company uses investors' capital and includes the debt. It is very important to compare companies in the same sector. If a company has a ROE that is much higher than its sector, be careful that something unusual isn't boosting the number (recent acquisitions, buying back stock, and so on).

Net margin. A company's net margin is simply net income divided by sales. What this tells you is how efficient the company is in wringing profits out of sales. Some industries (grocery stores, for example) have low net margins and must drive a lot of revenue to generate profits. Other industrial sectors have higher net margins thanks to the nature of the business (software, for example). Great companies beat sector averages and close competitors.

STOCK TIP

If you want to calculate key financial ratios or markers yourself, feel free to grab the latest statements and a calculator. However, you can find all of the key financial facts about a company online, often including historical numbers for reference.

Evaluating an Economic Moat's Width and Depth

All economic moats are not created equal. Some look wide, but may be shallow, while others are narrow, but deep. Great companies have economic moats that are wide and deep, which provide the best protection and are an indication that a company has a long-term future. There are several key characteristics to look at in evaluating a moat. Admittedly, some of this is somewhat subjective. You can find comments on these topics on most of the websites I mentioned in Chapter 3 (some may use the term economic advantage instead of economic moat):

Strong products. Few companies produce anything that is unique in the market, at least not for long if there is money to be made by the product. As soon as patents expire, generic drug makers duplicate leading products. When Apple introduced the iPhone in 2007 and the iPad a few years later, it created a whole new industry. There were other similar products on the market, but these two raised the bar so high competitors could only produce wannabes for a number of years. Eventually, competitors will match Apple's products, but in the meantime Apple is making money faster than it can count it. Apple has superior products and a hugely loyal customer base that is difficult to challenge. Great companies have products that competitors can't match and customers keep coming back. Either one (or both) is a wide and deep moat.

Locks out competitors. A strong economic moat can lock out competitors by cutting prices to the bone, yet still provide a profit to the company. A classic example of this is Wal-Mart, which has such efficient operations and massive buying power it can, and does, prove fatal to less-efficient competitors. Another way to lock out competitors is a high cost of entering the market. It takes a tremendous amount of money to start an airline and compete with existing carriers.

Locks in customers. An economic moat can protect a company's customer base by making it difficult or expensive for competitors to entice them away. One way to do this is make it difficult and/or expensive to switch. Cell phone providers are good at this by requiring most customers to sign a two-year agreement with a stiff penalty if they want out before two years. Banks and other financial companies want as much of your financial business (banking, loans, investing, insurance, and so on) as possible so moving your business would be difficult and inconvenient. Social media companies, such as Facebook, use networking to build a solid moat. You join because your friends and family joined and then a friend of yours joins, and so on. In early 2012, Facebook had 750 million users. Yes, a new social networking company may pop up (they do all the time), but it is hard to imagine one duplicating Facebook's success. However, people once said the same was true of MySpace (once the dominant social media site), which has faded from relevance.

Durability of an Economic Moat

How long will an economic moat retain is protection? This is almost impossible to know for sure, but by looking at the industry where the company competes, you may be able to make a guess. We are unlikely to give up toilet paper, food, or energy anytime soon. However, moats built on cutting-edge technology may not be sustainable. Unless companies keep innovating, technology alone is not strong protection—someone is always looking for and finding a better solution. Microsoft became an economic giant on the back of its operating system, which is widely considered far from the best, but is installed on some 90 percent of personal computers. Microsoft built on this positioning by introducing a suite of office technology tools that only (at that time) ran on its operating system and are ubiquitous in businesses around the world. Other companies with durable brand names such as Coke, General Mills, and General Electric have years of consumer confidence filling their moats.

No moat exists forever or is beyond breaching. All companies, even those with the strongest brand, customer base, and financial strength must work to maintain their economic advantage. If competitors find a crack in the protection, they will exploit it.

STOCK TIP

Analyzing a company may seem like a daunting task, and it can be. The key is to focus on the important concerns such as revenues, earnings, and cash flows. Then you will see a clear picture of the company's financial health.

The Next Step: Analyzing the Business

If you are satisfied the company has a large and sustainable economic advantage, it's time to move on to analyzing the business and coming up with a fair market value (intrinsic value). Two things to keep in mind: the intrinsic value is what the stock should be if it reflected the true value of the company, and it is also a moving target that will change as the company's financial fortunes change. Finding that number (stock price) will tell you whether the stock is a bargain, priced about right, or overpriced.

Value investors are looking for stocks that the market is pricing significantly below the intrinsic value. Growth investors may be happy with a stock price that is close to the intrinsic value, but the company still has much room for growth. If you are looking for a core stock that you hope will provide a higher stock price in the future and/or a steady stream of dividend income, the intrinsic value tells you if the stock is fairly priced.

Before I dive into valuation, let's look at some of the more popular stock ratios.

Using Ratios in Analysis

You will hear and read a lot about ratios, or multiples, as they are sometimes called. A quick glance at a stock on Morningstar will reveal many different ratios: price earnings ratio, price to sales ratio, price to book ratio, and so on. While some ratios provide a hint about the company's intrinsic value, most of them are based on the stock's current price. That price can be overstated in the case of a hot growth stock or understated for stocks in languishing sectors. While they have some value to the long-term investors, they reflect the market's view of the stock today or for the short term. They tell us little or nothing about the future value of the company.

Earnings Per Share (EPS)

Earnings per share is a popular metric and the basis for other ratios. You take the company's net earnings and divide that number by the outstanding shares. (EPS = net earnings/outstanding shares)

The EPS is helpful in comparing one company to another, assuming they are in the same industry, but it doesn't tell you whether it's a good stock to buy or what the market thinks of it. For that information, you need to look at some ratios.

Before I move on, you should note that there are three types of EPS numbers:

- Trailing EPS—last year's numbers and the only actual EPS
- Current EPS—this year's numbers, which are still projections
- Forward EPS—future numbers, which are obviously projections

Price Earnings Ratio (P/E)

The price earnings ratio is the most popular of all stock ratios, at least with the media. You calculate the P/E by dividing the stock's price by its EPS (P/E = Stock Price/EPS).

For example, a company with a share price of $40 and an EPS of 2 would have a P/E of 2 ($40/2 = 20). This means that investors are willing to pay $20 in the stock's price for every dollar of earnings, which would put this stock in the overpriced category if others in its sector are trading at a P/E of 12.

What does P/E tell you? The P/E gives you an idea of what the market is willing to pay for the company's earnings. The higher the P/E the more the market is willing to pay for the company's earnings. Some investors read a high P/E as an overpriced stock, and that may be the case. However, it can also indicate the market has high hopes for this stock's future and has bid up the price. It almost certainly means this is not the time to buy the stock.

Conversely, a low P/E may indicate a "vote of no confidence" by the market or it could mean this is a sleeper that the market has overlooked.

What is the "right" P/E? There is no correct answer to this question, because part of the answer depends on your willingness to pay for earnings. Some investors may consider a company with a high P/E overpriced, and they may be correct. A high P/E may be a signal that traders have pushed a stock's price beyond the point where any reasonable near-term growth is probable.

However, a high P/E may also be a strong vote of confidence that the company still has strong growth prospects in the future, which should mean an even higher stock price. Most long-term investors shy away from stocks that post high P/Es, because it may indicate there is little room left for growth in price without a much higher risk that the market will also become nervous and abandon the stock, causing the price to fall dramatically.

Compare a stock's P/E to its sector and competitors to get an idea how similar companies are being priced. However, the P/E changes every day the stock closes at a new price and quarterly when new earnings are reported.

Other ratios such as price to book, price to sales, dividend yield, and others are often used to value stocks. While these can tell you whether the stock is trading above its sector or the whole market, they tell you nothing helpful about the value of the business. Ratios are helpful when buying or selling for the short-term because price is more important than value. However, for the long-term investor, value is more important.

MARKET RISK

Too many investors become hung up on analyzing all the dozens of ratios generated from the company's financial statements. Bogging down in details is a way to lose focus on the objective of identifying great companies and buying their stock at a great price.

Intrinsic Value Using Discounted Cash Flows

While ratios offer some information about what the market considers a fair price today, those numbers can be distorted by many factors. The most common method of arriving at the intrinsic value of a stock is using the discounted cash flows method. Discounted valuation models are used to price a number of different assets. The model that most stock analysts use is the discounted cash flows method. It is a complicated process that involves some math and making some assumptions about things such as future revenue, free cash flow, and more. Don't become discouraged by the math and projections, this is a tool you can use.

Before I dig deeper into the discounted cash flow model, it is important that you understand the reasoning behind using this process and why it is the favored method of most stock investors.

Understanding Discounting and Future Value

Money has a time value that must be considered with any investment, whether it is stocks, real estate, or something else. The time value of money simply stated is that a dollar today is worth more than a promised dollar in a year. The reason is that you have the dollar today and you can invest it to earn a profit. Equally important, you have it and there is no risk that you won't have it, as compared with the risk of a dollar promised in the future. Many things can happen in a year, which could mean you would not receive the promised dollar or other bad circumstances.

If a dollar today is worth more than a dollar in one year, why would I choose a possible future benefit over a real (dollar) benefit I have in my hand? One way to address this problem is to acknowledge the time value of money. To entice me to wait a year, I must be rewarded. At the very least, in one year I should receive the equivalent of one dollar today, plus a premium for risking the wait.

The discounted cash flow method for valuing stocks rests on this principle, but from a different perspective. The simple description of discounted cash flows is that a stock is worth the sum of future discounted cash flows. If you project a company is going to have future free cash flows of 5 percent more than the previous year, you can calculate what each of those cash flows will be (starting with $100) at the end of …

> Year one = $105
>
> Year two = $110.25
>
> Year three = $115.76
>
> Year four = $121.55
>
> Year five = $127.63

However, thanks to the time value of money, you know that each year's cash flows must be discounted and the farther out the cash flows the greater the discount.

The discounted cash flow model uses other projections and estimates to arrive at a fair market value for the stock. This is the method preferred by most stock analysts. If you are clever in math and confident you can predict future cash flows, revenues, and other variables, there are many places on the internet that will show you how to make these calculations.

Here is the basic model used by many analysts (there are many variations of this formula):

$$PV = CF1 / (1+k) + CF2 / (1+k)2 + \ldots [TCF / (k-g)] / (1+k)n-1$$

Where:

PV = present value

CFi = cash flow in year i

k = discount rate

TCF = the terminal year cash flow

g = growth rate assumption in perpetuity beyond terminal year

n = the number of periods in the valuation model including the terminal year

(This model is from Investopedia.com.)

The Weakness of the Discounted Cash Flow Model

The weakness of the discounted cash flow model is you (and me). The model only works if you have realistic estimates to include on future cash flows, estimated future revenues, how much risk is involved, industry analysis, and so on.

There are discounted cash flow calculators on the internet that simply require you to enter some estimates and the program will calculate the number for you. The outcome is only as good as the data you enter. Whether you do the calculations manually or use one of the online calculators, the outcome will still be tainted by the estimates you enter. It is possible to find estimates for many of the variables on the internet; however, it is not always possible to verify how the author arrived at these conclusions. Among industry professionals there are often wide differences in estimates and risk factors.

The Strengths of the Discounted Cash Flow Model

The model produces actionable numbers if the inputs are from professional analysts who study the market and study the stock you are researching. The intrinsic value is still subjective because of the estimates, and other professional analysts may see the company differently. However, your best bet for finding a reliable estimate of a stock's intrinsic value is from an expert. It has been my experience that Morningstar provides the best and most consistent information on a stock's intrinsic value.

STOCK TIP

Researching stocks and companies is easy on the internet, but be very careful of the sources you use. Stick with names and sources you know and trust. The websites listed in Chapter 3 are trustworthy, I believe, and I have no financial interest in them except for the one indicated as such. If a commentator is touting a stock, he or she should disclose if they have any financial interest in the stock or stand to gain if the price rises.

To access this expertise, you must pay their subscription fee for premium membership. The cost is surprisingly affordable considering the amount and quality of information they provide. Morningstar offers a 14-day free trial (you must subscribe, but can opt out during the 14 days at no cost). For less than a couple of lattes per week, you can have access to some of the best minds in the business. If you don't like the service, you can cancel. There are other subscription services that may be as good or better, but Morningstar is the one I know and recommend. Morningstar also offers detailed descriptions of how discounted cash flows are calculated for those wanting to do their own math.

Alternative to Discounted Cash Flow Method

What do you use if you don't want to or can't use the discounted cash flow method of valuing a stock? There are other methods for valuing a stock (not valuing the company). The most popular alternative uses various multiples to compare the price of one stock to a comparable stock. The price earnings ratio (P/E) is the most popular multiple for these comparisons.

The procedure is not unlike using comparables to appraise a house for sale. In that case, the real estate agent finds comparable houses in the area that have sold recently and uses that information to arrive at a price for your house. The idea is that comparable assets should sell for similar prices. The same process is used for stocks with the P/E being the common factor.

For example, if you are considering Stock A, which has a P/E of 12, look for comparable stocks (same industry, same size, and so on). If you find three other comparables with P/Es respectively of 18, 17, and 20, you could conclude that Stock A is underpriced because investors are willing to pay more for the earnings of the other three companies.

You can use the P/E formula to find the price based on comparable stocks. Continuing with Stock A, you could average the three comparables to get a target P/E of, say, 18.5. If Stock A had earnings of \$2.50 per share, you could calculate a stock price of \$46.25 per share (earnings – 2.50 × P/E – 18.5 = 46.25 per-share price). This is just an approximation, but it should put Stock A on a comparable basis with the three comparable stocks.

This strategy has several flaws, including that the P/E is not always the most reliable of value gauges. The process depends on the three comparables being priced correctly, and there is no guarantee of that. Its biggest flaw is that the process tells you nothing of the future value of the company or the stock. If you use this method, and many investors do, you will need to watch the stock more closely and continually measure it against comparables. However, it does not require you to estimate anything or consider multiple variables, which is why it is so popular.

This method is best used for a quick decision on whether the stock is underpriced or overpriced. Although you can arrive at a stock price based on the P/E formula, it is not nearly as accurate as the discounted cash flow method. You can also use other key ratios, and all of these can be found on the websites I mentioned in Chapter 3 and others.

Other key ratios you can use in valuation include the following:

- Price/Book—Value market places on book value (share price/book value per share
- Price/Sales—Value market places on sales (share price/ sales per share
- Price/Cash Flow—Value market places on cash flow (share price/cash flow per share)
- Dividend Yield—Shareholder yield from dividends (annual dividends per share/price per share)

In the end, you will have to decide which method is for you. There is no rule against using both. Whether you calculate your own discounted cash flows or use a service like Morningstar, make sure you have the best guess available on the variables the formula needs. Either way, make a conscious decision to buy a stock based on the valuation method of your choice and not a "feeling" for the stock.

When to Buy or Sell

For the long-term investor there are only three important stock prices: the fair market price, the price they pay, and the price they sell. All other price movement by a stock is really not relevant and may confuse or frighten an investor into making a hasty decision. You should never buy a stock without a plan to sell the stock. When you work from a plan, you are less likely to be distracted by market news that is only relevant to stock prices for a few days. If you have a plan, you're less likely to sell during a downturn or buy during an upturn. Although it may seem overly simple, if you buy at the right price and sell at the right price you will make money investing in stocks. It's as simple as that. However, nothing is ever very simple where money is involved. The stock market is notorious for letting emotions drive stock prices in crazy directions. Long-term investors hope the stocks they buy will grow and add value year after year. However, things change and companies either adapt or they cease being great companies and you must reconsider your ownership. Because the future is unknown, the best you can do is identify great companies you want to own, find a price that fairly represents the company's value, and hope for an opportunity to buy below that price. In the end, investing in stocks for the long-term is hoping for the best and preparing for the worst.

Don't Follow the Crowd

Despite all the news about computer trading programs that use sophisticated software to make buy and sell decisions, there are still humans involved in the daily ebb and flow of stock market prices. Humans, many of whom want to be as unemotional as a computer program, are still driven by two basic human emotions: fear and greed. When these emotions take over the market, logic is replaced.

These powerful emotions can spread and infect otherwise rational people. There are many examples of what happens when emotions overrun logic. The classic example is the dot.com boom of the late 1990s that drove the stock market to put insanely high prices on companies that were little more than a rough outline written on a napkin. Companies that had no products or services, much less profits, were bid up to unreasonably high prices. In March 2000, the stock market woke up and realized most of its newly found darlings would never produce a usable product or service.

As investors fled the market, indexes such as the *Nasdaq Composite* fell into what appeared to be a bottomless hole. In a very short time, it lost more than half of its value. *The Dow Jones Industrial Average* (the Dow) and the *S&P 500 Index* also suffered severe drops. During a short period, hundreds of billions of dollars worth of value disappeared from the stock market. The inflated values of the tech stocks burst like the balloon they were.

DEFINITION

The S&P 500 Index tracks the leading 500 companies on all exchanges. It is considered a proxy for the whole stock market.

The Dow follows 30 leading companies and is the emotional bellwether of the stock market. Members of the Dow are the market leaders.

The Nasdaq Composite follows more than 3,000 companies. It is often used as a proxy for the technology sector.

Following the Buyers

When greed overtakes the market, traders no longer care what price they are paying for stock. They feel they can ignore valuation and any other logic in favor of a strategy that says there will always be someone else who is willing to pay you more than you paid for a stock. As the stock market becomes excited about the possibility of rapidly rising prices, amateur investors decide this is a time they want to invest in the stock market. Unfortunately, they lack the tools or strategy of professional short-term traders who welcome them to the market as a new source of profits—also known as dumb money.

During the dot.com boom, *day-trading* became a new career for many people who left their jobs and began speculating in the stock market. Media stories of cabdrivers turned day-traders only fueled the interest of more people wanting to get in on the easy money. Even among professional day-traders, it's a risky business at best with a high failure rate. For newcomers with little experience and minimal training, there was a slaughter.

This pattern repeats itself time and time again. The lesson for long-term stock investors is to stick with buying great companies at great prices.

DEFINITION

Day-trading is the rapid buying and selling of large blocks of stock in hopes of profiting on small price changes. Day-traders may make 100 or more trades a day, sometimes only holding a stock for a few minutes or seconds before selling.

Following the Sellers

Of the two emotions, fear is much more powerful than greed. This has been demonstrated time and time again with a variety of studies, but can be summarized with the following point: If I told you there was an 80 percent chance an investment would make money, most people would be favorably inclined to consider the investment. However, if I said there's a 20 percent chance you will lose money with this investment, most people would say that is too risky and decline the offer. Yet this is obviously the same investment simply referenced two different ways. Fear of loss is a tremendous power that often overcomes common sense and causes long-term investors to make dangerous mistakes.

When the market is in a steep decline, for whatever reason, the media often notes how many people are cashing out of stocks and stock mutual funds. The deeper the decline, the more people flee to the supposed safety of cash or bonds. When prices are falling, investors forget that owning stocks is a long-term strategy. The stock market always has periods of decline and periods of strong growth. This is a reason stocks are not good choices to meet financial goals that have deadlines fewer than five years out.

During the market decline beginning in 2007 and finally bottoming in March 2008, thousands of investors sold their stocks and fled to the sidelines. As the market began a slow recovery in 2009 and 2010, some of the investors cautiously came back into stocks. Many others waited until they were sure the market wasn't going to dip again before returning to stocks. The unfortunate outcome of these reactions is that stockholders sold as prices were declining and bought back in as prices rose.

Smart investors took one of two routes during this period: they rode out the market and waited for prices to return or they bought when prices were low and added to their holdings. Both strategies meant it was very likely they came out of the decline in 2012 in a much better position than the investors who sold as prices fell and bought as prices rose.

A Planned Approach to Buying and Selling

Successful investors in the stock market have a plan for each stock they buy. The process starts with identifying the stock and determining a fair market (intrinsic) price for the stock. You then analyze the company's economic advantage (economic moat) to determine if it is wide and deep enough to provide protection for the foreseeable future. Having satisfied yourself that you have a realistic fair market price that accurately values the company and includes an economic moat, your next step is to decide what the top price is you want to pay.

Margin of Error

No matter how hard you work at determining a fair market price, you need to allow for the possibility that you could be wrong or a service like Morningstar could also be wrong. After all, the price was derived from a formula that relied on estimates of future cash flows. If you used the comparable method of valuation, your price may be more at risk of being wrong. Either way, smart investors provide a cushion in the price they are willing to pay for a stock. This cushion is called the margin of error. Here's how it works:

For example, you have done your due diligence and are convinced the stock has a strong economic moat and are comfortable with a fair market price of $30 per share. However, you want some protection against the possibility that $30 a share may not be the right price. You discount the $30 price by a percentage to your new price. How much of a discount is a matter of personal preference, but many investors use 15 to 20 percent. A more conservative investor might choose 20 percent or more, while other investors might choose the lower discount.

Assuming you felt 20 percent is the margin of error you choose, your target price would then be $24 per share ($30 \times .20 = 6$). That is the most you will pay for this stock. As you can see, this conservative approach may eliminate many stocks from consideration. The patient (and successful) long-term investor will wait for the stock's price to drop to this level before buying, and if it doesn't drop to the target, the investor doesn't buy. The temptation, especially after a lot of hard work, is to buy the stock even if it is not at or below the target price. Of course, this defeats the purpose of the margin of error and your buy becomes much more risky.

A smaller margin of error may bring the target price closer to where the stock is currently trading, but you must accept the possibility that you may pay too much for the stock. If you pay too much, it may be difficult to realize the level of return you anticipated. Growth and value investors have somewhat different views of this process, which I discuss in the next section.

STOCK TIP

There are various stock market orders that will help you buy the stock at the price you want. They tell your broker at what price to buy the stock so you don't have to watch the market constantly to get the price you want. More about orders in Chapter 10.

Creating a Buy Plan

Before you buy a stock, you should be able to state, in writing, the reasons for buying. This is known in the business as a "buy case." A buy case is a simple, to-the-point summary of why this stock makes sense for your portfolio. It covers important points about the company and the stock and forces you to do your homework before investing.

Your buy case will come in handy if the stock takes a tumble. It provides a reminder of why you bought the stock and a checklist to see if the company still meets your standards. Follow this procedure or one similar to it and you'll avoid buying (or selling) as an emotional response. Here are some points your buy plan should cover (you can add others):

What does the company do? If you can't explain the major business activity of the company in two or three sentences, you shouldn't be investing in it.

What part of the economy does this business serve, and is it growing? Does the company own a large share of that market? What is its competitive advantage (economic moat)?

Is the company riding a demographic or economic trend that has long-term implications? Companies that serve retirement needs of baby boomers have a 76 million plus market. Companies that define their market too narrowly limit their potential growth.

What do you see that makes you believe the company has room for sustained growth? Why do you believe the company is in a good position to grow and the stock is not priced to reflect this potential? Maybe the stock has been beat up because of some bad company news you judge to be temporary. Maybe the sector is out of favor and generally depressed. Whatever the reason, you should have a reasonable answer for why the stock price is lower than it could or should be.

Is the company financially sound? Does it have solid earnings growth? Low debt for its industry? Strong, free cash flow?

When you have built a convincing buy case (at a certain price), you are ready to invest. Retain the buy case and review it at least once a year or more often if the stock takes a big hit to see if any of your assumptions or conclusions have changed.

When you build a buy case before buying a stock, you force yourself to make a rational decision. Investing on instinct is the same as guessing; sometimes you'll be right and sometimes you'll be wrong—not a great way to a solid financial future.

When to Buy Different Types of Stocks

Any stock you buy should follow the same guidelines listed previously and the same pricing procedure detailed in Chapter 6. However, there are some differences in the types of stocks you buy and the timing of the purchases. Every investor needs to own a group of core stocks, which are large, market-leading household name stocks. Some investors satisfy this requirement with an investment in index mutual funds. Exchange traded funds that track major market indexes will work also. However, this is a book about investing in individual stocks, so I discuss this requirement in that context.

STOCK TIP

Exchange traded funds and index mutual funds track stock market indexes that often cover a broad section of the stock market. They are a low-cost way to "buy" the market.

When to Buy Core Stocks

Core stocks are the bedrock of your portfolio. These are the stocks that inspire confidence in their ability to earn a decent return, but also to weather stormy markets better than most of the market. When times are uncertain, investors turn to core stocks for their stability. For example, Coca-Cola dropped during the financial crisis that began in 2008, but it never dropped as far as the whole market and rebounded ahead of the market.

Core stocks should be your first buy if you are building a portfolio from scratch and your next buy if you don't own several core stocks already. Not every large stock qualifies as a core stock and even some previous market leaders, while still large, have lost the edge that made them great companies. You still must do your research and not just buy one of the components of the Dow Jones Industrial Average (the Dow).

When to Buy Growth Stocks

One of the best times, in general, to buy growth stocks is during a market dip. If you have done your homework and believe the company is a solid prospect, buying during a market downturn may be a good idea. Investors generally don't like growth stocks that don't grow or don't grow fast enough. If you are convinced the company's growth is just temporarily stalled, consider buying when others are selling.

Growth stocks can be added as your resources and opportunities allow. Like all of your stock purchases, the buying price is critical. However, growth investors are often lax with their research and assume strong growth will overcome any mistakes in the price paid. Wouldn't you rather see that growth adds value to your holdings rather than have to correct your mistake?

When to Buy Value Stocks

Successful value investors (and there are some that buy nothing but value stocks) are rigid in their price requirements. They have a plan and stick to it, even if that means they must pass on 10 stocks, before they find one that meets their standards. A value investor is convinced (by her research) that the company is solid and under-appreciated by the stock market. Patience and persistence define value investors.

Have a Plan to Sell Stocks

Successful investors have a plan to sell each stock they own. This plan covers market circumstances such as a significant drop or rise in the stock's price. It also details when you might want to sell for more personal reasons. Either way, the sell plan is in place so if circumstances change rapidly, you don't have to make an uninformed decision. This is not a long document, but rather a series of short statements, something like: "If the stock drops X percent, I will (sell or add to my holdings)." "If the stock rises to $X, I will sell Y number of shares or all shares." You get the idea and know what fits your personal financial situations. Here are some reasons for selling you may want to include in your plan:

Risk tolerance reached. You bought a company that looked like a steady, growing concern, but instead the stock has turned out to be a rollercoaster ride. For whatever reason, this stock is just too volatile for your nerves. Dump this firecracker and replace it with a stock that will let you sleep at night.

You need cash. An unexpected major bill can sabotage anyone's budget. Using a stock, especially one that is underperforming, to solve a financial emergency is another reason to sell. However, take a close look at your personal finances. An emergency cash fund that is not tied up in investments is recommended to avoid, except in extreme cases, liquidating stocks to pay bills.

Moral, ethical conflicts. More and more investors are becoming concerned about the social, environmental, ethical, and moral standards of the companies they own. You may decide that a company you own has practices or products that conflict with your social, religious, or moral beliefs. There is no better reason to sell if that is important to you.

The grass is greener. There is nothing wrong with dumping an underwhelming stock for a company that offers better returns. Long-term investors should avoid dumping carefully researched stock because the price has slumped. If the company still passes your buy case, look (and think) before you leap. The attractive stock you don't own may be a flash on the market, only to fall hard.

MARKET RISK

It is easy to suffer "buyer's remorse" after making a major
stock purchase. All of a sudden, you doubt your decision and
some other stock looks more appealing. Remember your buy
case and refer to it to remind yourself why you bought the
stock you did.

You've reached your goal. It worked. Your plan to reach that financial goal, whether it is retirement or getting a child to college, is
finally here. Now is the time to start systematically liquidating
those stocks you've tagged for this goal.

The stock drops by X percent. Your sell plan should address this
situation. You have several basic choices. You can sell all the
stock you own and move on to another stock. You can sell part
of the stock you own, which is a tactic to take some money out
of the stock, but hold on to some shares in case they rebound.

The company flounders. This is your signal to sell. You bought
the company because of its fundamentals and its business plan.
When something changes and the company loses its way, you
re-examine whether it is the same company or not. The company
may find itself out of step with its industry and loses its leader-
ship position.

When a stock is overvalued. Can there be too much of a good
thing? There certainly can in the market. When stocks are
pushed way past their true value, they are often set up for a fall.
Selling an overvalued stock is certainly preferable to buying an
overvalued stock. Just be prepared to watch it keep going up after
you sell, as happens sometimes. Don't second-guess yourself; it
could have more easily gone the other way.

Rebalancing your portfolio. You have decided that the best allocation for your circumstances is 60 percent stocks, 30 percent
bonds, and 10 percent cash in your portfolio. Good fortune has
smiled on you and your stocks, which are now valued at 75 percent of your portfolio. As tempting as it might be to stay there,
your best move is to rebalance your portfolio by selling off some
of your stocks and bringing the percentages back into alignment.

Taxes and Investing

A major concern for all investors is to hold down the expenses of investing, which reduce your gains. Expenses fall into two categories: direct investing expenses (broker commissions, for example) and taxes. I will cover investing expenses in Chapter 10. Taxes that you pay or avoid in investing are controlled by when and how you buy and sell stocks. There are two major forms of taxation on investors: capital gains and dividends. However, before I discuss taxes directly, there are strategies to avoid some taxes and defer others until much later.

Choosing to Defer Taxes

Taxes are a part of our lives and there is no getting around that fact. That said, there is no legal or moral reason for you to pay any more than you are legally required to pay. With some planning and foreknowledge, you can keep your tax bill for your stock investing to a minimum.

This is not about tax dodging or evasion, nor is it a substitute for competent tax counsel for complex tax issues. I have an agreement with my tax attorney friends—I don't practice tax law and they don't sue me. So far, it's working out pretty well.

The best strategy is to place as much of your stock investing in a tax-qualified account as possible. Tax-qualified accounts, such as 401(k) plans and the various IRA accounts, allow your investment to grow tax-deferred (or tax-free in the case of Roth accounts). This means that as long as the investment and any income, such as dividends or profits from sales, remains in the tax-qualified account, you pay no taxes on the gains. In regular tax-qualified accounts, you don't pay income or other taxes until you begin withdrawing money, presumably in retirement. This allows more of your money and earnings to remain and benefit from compounding. There are a variety of rules and regulations you must follow (and even more for Roth accounts) regarding withdrawals. In most cases, if you wait until you are at least 59½, you avoid any penalties. I can't cover all the issues with qualified accounts, but it is well worth your efforts to learn more from competent tax advisers.

MARKET RISK

Tax rates are subject to change and the tax code even more so. Don't make any tax decisions without consulting a qualified tax adviser who is current on investment tax regulations.

Taxes and Investing in Stocks

There are two main ways income or profits from investing in stocks may be taxed:

- Capital gains tax
- Dividend income tax

Capital gains tax. A capital gain occurs when you sell an asset for a profit. That asset could be a house, land, machinery, stock, or a bond. When that happens, you have experienced a capital gain. You figure the capital gains tax on the difference between your "basis" in the stock and the sales price. This difference is your profit or loss. The basis is usually what you paid for the stock. However, if you inherit the stock, the basis is the price of the stock on the day the owner died.

If the difference between the basis and the sales price is negative—in other words, you lost money—you have a capital loss, which you can use to offset capital gains in some cases.

There are two types of capital gains:

- Long-term capital gains
- Short-term capital gains

It is very important to understand the difference and why one is better than the other:

Long-term capital gains. You must hold the stock at least one full year to qualify for the long-term capital gains rates. This is extremely important and I encourage you to make absolutely sure by holding the stock one year and a day at least. The tax on a long-term capital gain is currently 15 percent if you are in the 25 percent income tax bracket or higher and just 5 percent if you are in the 15 percent or lower tax bracket.

Short-term capital gains. If you hold a stock less than one year before selling it, the IRS classifies the sale as a short-term capital gain and taxes the profit as ordinary income. This means you could pay 25 percent or much higher of your profit in taxes.

Unless there is a compelling reason, hold on to the stock long enough to qualify for the long-term capital gains rates.

In some cases, a short-term or long-term capital loss can offset all or part of the tax.

Dividend tax. Companies that distribute profits through dividends create a taxable event for you. The IRS taxes dividends at 15 percent; however, it is subject to change. Otherwise, dividends may be considered ordinary income and taxed at your current rate. There is not much you can do to avoid some tax on dividends, unless you hold your stock in a qualified retirement plan and have a dividend reinvestment plan.

Building a Portfolio

You absolutely need a plan for buying and selling stocks; however, each of those decisions should fit into a broader plan for your entire portfolio. Buying individual companies is the way to find great stocks, but how those stocks fit into your total holdings is as important as the stocks you buy. When you take the idea of core, growth, and value stocks and combine them with small, mid, and large sizes, you quickly see there are many possible combinations. Layered on top of those choices are the industrial sectors every company belongs to and you have many possible outcomes. Making sense of all of these possible combinations is the plan you build for a portfolio that fits your financial goals and risk tolerance. That plan, called asset allocation, helps you weather the volatility of the stock market and avoid some of the risks.

Understanding Asset Allocation

Asset allocation is the thoughtful use of assets (investment capital) to balance risk and reward across your holdings. Typically, investors have three classes of assets: securities, fixed-income assets, and cash. This is where you should start. More sophisticated forms of asset allocation add other classes of assets such as real estate, precious metals, and so on. The vast majority of investors need only concern themselves with the three basic classes. Diversification is often used as a synonym for asset allocation, but it has a more narrow focus.

Asset Allocation and Diversification

Asset allocation and diversification are both strategies to reduce risk. Asset allocation involves how all three asset classes work together to manage risk and improve returns. Diversification refers to how you structure each class for the best results. For example, asset allocation looks at the percentage of each asset class in your portfolio (stocks—60 percent; bonds—20 percent; cash—20 percent). Diversification considers how you spread your stock investments over several industrial sectors (tech— 10 percent; financial—35 percent; retail—15 percent; consumer goods—15 percent; utilities—25 percent). To avoid extra explanations, I will simply refer to asset allocation and you can assume I am including diversification as part of the process.

The Importance of Asset Allocation

As "jargony" as asset allocation sounds, it is incredibly important to your success as an investor in the stock market. Many studies have confirmed that finding the correct asset allocation is as or more important than the securities you buy. This means even if you do the best job of picking stocks and other assets, you still may not achieve the return you expected if your asset allocation is wrong.

Here's why this is true. Stocks and bonds (the fixed-income asset class in most cases) frequently move in different directions. Economic circumstances that may drive down stock prices tend to increase the value of bonds and when stocks are rising, the value of bonds may suffer. If you have a good balance, your portfolio may not suffer as much if one asset class drops, because it is likely the other will rise. The opposite is also true: if stocks take off on a steep rise, you may not achieve the same results with a portfolio balanced with all three asset classes, because bonds may fall in value.

This is the balance between risk and reward that asset allocation brings to your portfolio. Because the future is unknowable, your best chance of success is to build your portfolio with an asset allocation that achieves the balance between risk and reward that is comfortable for you. There is no one "correct" asset allocation. Investors must decide for themselves what makes the most sense for their circumstances and tolerance for risk.

STOCK TIP

Many of the websites I mentioned in Chapter 3 have tools that will let you view how a portfolio of stocks, bonds, and cash may perform as you change the percentages of each asset class. This is helpful in giving you an idea if a particular portfolio is the best for you.

Those Other Two Asset Classes: Fixed Income and Cash

Although this is a book about investing in stocks, it is impossible to talk about portfolios and asset allocation without touching on fixed income and cash. Making good decisions about these two asset classes is important to your success. They both play a role in the balance between risk and reward.

Why Include Cash?

Cash is included as an asset class because it is the steadiest and most liquid of all investment vehicles. That may seem obvious, but running short of cash in your investment portfolio may mean scrambling to pay for an opportunity you identify that works for your strategy (not a tip from your neighbor on a hot stock). For example, a stock you have been watching for some time finally dips below your target price. Having part or all of the cash readily available may let you make the purchase without disrupting the rest of your plan or dipping into savings, which is different from the cash you have for investing. Your cash account is where you park money waiting to invest or reinvest if you have sold a security. At times, it may be higher than the normal percentage you have allocated if you are parking money for re-investment. Cash doesn't usually pay much in the way of a return. In periods of very low interest rates, cash may not keep up with inflation, so it is actually losing some value. You can park your cash in the following places:

- Bank accounts
- Bank certificates of deposit
- Money market mutual funds
- Stock brokerage accounts
- Very short-term Treasury bills

Fixed-Income Securities (Bonds)

Fixed-income securities provide a steady income or a fixed return at maturity. For my purposes, they refer to bonds, although you could also use bank certificates of deposit. Bonds and bank CDs are debt instruments; you are lending money to the bond issuer or bank in exchange for a stated return. Bonds are the preferred fixed-income asset class for asset allocation purposes because they come in a variety of maturities and with varying degrees of risk. Bonds pay a fixed interest rate until maturity when all of your investment is returned. Bonds are rated for their security by outside companies. The more risky a rating company believes the bond is the higher interest rate it must pay. There are basically three issuers of bonds ranked in terms of general safety:

U.S. Treasury issues. Treasuries, as they are known, are the gold standard for virtually risk-free investing, because they are backed by the "full faith" of the U.S. government. The Treasury issues bills, notes, and bonds with maturities ranging from days to 30 years. For conservative investors, these are the securities of choice. The absolute safety of your principal comes with a price: Treasuries pay the lowest return of all bonds. Income from Treasuries is exempt from state and local taxes, but not federal income tax.

Other government entities. Frequently known as a municipal bond or muni, these bonds are issued by governmental entities other than the federal government. They also have a variety of maturities. Income from municipal bonds is low, but not as low as Treasuries. They are not as safe as Treasuries and some may be risky, depending on the financial health of the issuer. Municipal bonds are exempt from federal income tax and, in some cases, may be exempt from state and local taxes.

Corporate bonds. Companies issue bonds rather than sell more stock and dilute the ownership. The bond market is usually a better place to borrow long term than banks or other lenders. Corporate bonds range from very secure to highly risky, so know what you are doing before you buy a bond.

Bonds would require a whole book to explain in detail, but this brief overview will place them in context for our discussion on portfolios.

 MARKET RISK

Buying individual bonds can be tricky for the uninformed—except for Treasuries. Many investors use a bond index mutual fund or a bond index exchange traded fund to meet their bond asset class requirement.

Timing Is Everything

Building a portfolio that fits a particular asset allocation begins with an understanding of how much time you have to reach your financial goal—for most of us, the top goal is building a secure retirement. If you were (are) smart, you started saving for retirement as soon as you started your first adult job. Of course, most of us weren't thinking about retirement as young adults. Starting young and staying with a program to build a secure retirement is the best way to reach that goal. If your employer offers a retirement program such as a 401(k), sign up on day one and contribute what you can, but certainly up to the maximum percentage your employer will match.

For people still 30 or 40 years away from retirement, it makes sense to be as aggressive (but not crazy) with your portfolio as you are comfortable given your tolerance for risk. If you make a mistake or the market turns against your aggressive stocks, you have time to recover. However, if you have fewer than 10 years before retirement, you will want to be much more conservative with your stock investments. At this stage of life, preserving what you have becomes more important than hitting aggressive growth goals. Think of asset allocation like an accelerator on a car. When you are young, you drive fast and take chances. As you grow older, you slow down and become more cautious. This is how your investing should work also.

How to Build a Portfolio That Fits You

Building a portfolio that fits you starts with an understanding of the relative risk associated with the possible combinations of asset classes. Using this understanding, you can fit the pieces together to build a portfolio that addresses your financial goals and is within your tolerance for risk. You should never buy a stock(s) or put together a portfolio that keeps you awake at night because it is too risky. Each asset class, with the exception of cash, has its own risk concerns. If you keep your cash in one of the places previously mentioned, you should not have to worry about its safety.

Fixed-Income (Bonds) Asset Class

To take advantage of the tendency of bonds to move in the opposite direction of stocks, you should use bonds for this asset class. Bonds come in a variety of risk profiles, maturities, and returns. Treasuries are the safest, followed by well-rated municipal bonds and corporate bonds. Except for Treasuries and all other bonds, there is not a sharp line between risk of corporate and municipal bonds. A highly rated corporate bond will be less risky (and still may pay more) than a poorly rated municipal.

The longer the maturity of all bonds, the higher interest rate it must offer, because more time means more chances for events to negatively impact bonds. The higher the risk (lower ratings), the more interest bonds must pay to compensate buyers for the risk. An aggressive bond would be a mid- to low-rated corporate bond, while a conservative bond would be a Treasury or highly rated municipal bond. Bonds are referenced in the portfolios that follow, but only to show how they fit into the asset allocation.

Stocks Asset Class

As a broad rule, stocks are more risky than bonds. As with most generalities, it is easy to poke holes in a flat statement. Top-quality companies (core stocks) are less risky than very poorly rated corporate bonds. However, within the continuum that includes all stocks, there are some that are more risky than others. Growth stocks tend to be more risky than core stocks. Value stocks may or may not be more risky than growth stocks.

The size of the company matters a great deal when assessing the risk of the stock. Small company stocks are more risky than large company stocks. Stocks in certain industrial sectors may be more risky than stocks in other sectors. Tech stocks are often more risky than other industrial sectors because technology can change quickly—today's leader can be tomorrow's also-ran. However, economic circumstances can move almost any industrial sector into the risky column. For example, during the housing collapse that began in 2007, homebuilders took a devastating blow as did major appliance makers and so on.

When you put company size and industrial sector together, you get pieces of the allocation puzzle that fit in specific slots. For example, small tech companies are generally considered risky, even when the sector is doing well, so they may have a place in an aggressive portfolio. Very large, well-diversified companies (core stocks) work in almost every portfolio to some extent (more so in conservative allocations; less so in aggressive ones).

STOCK TIP

Many stock screens let you select small- and mid-size core stocks. I only consider core stocks that are large or very large, because those companies have the greatest stability and endurance. Going smaller in core stocks doesn't make much sense to me.

Diversification and Stocks

In addition to considering size and type of stock (core, growth, value), you need to be certain that stocks you add to your holdings are diversified. Diversification ensures the same economic forces do not affect your stocks. For example, high interest rates hurt makers of big-ticket items such as cars and housing. On the other hand, utilities and consumer staples (think toilet paper) do not drop as far as other stocks during an economic downturn—they also do not rise as fast or as far when the economy is booming. These stocks are called noncyclical or defensive because they help smooth out the peaks and valleys of the market.

Portfolio Models

Following are three models of portfolios that illustrate the range of asset allocation possibilities. Although they range from aggressive to conservative, there is not a point where investors switch from one to another. The transition is more like a sliding scale that begins with aggressive and is modified over time as it moves toward conservative. It is important to note that you do not have to start with an aggressive portfolio. I am assuming the aggressive portfolio is for a young investor who is moving through her life and modifying as she ages. Many investors don't become serious about investing until they are older and more established (and have investment capital). If that fits you and you want to start very aggressively, that's fine as long as you fully understand the risks. On the other hand, if you are 25 years old and are only comfortable with a conservative approach, that's fine also. Where you start is up to you.

The following three portfolios simply illustrate possibilities. I used real stocks in these models, but chose not to name them. I don't want to suggest any specific investment, but rather illustrate the concept.

An Aggressive Portfolio

An aggressive portfolio is designed to significantly beat the market with your return. To have a chance to hit your mark, you need a portfolio that is sufficiently aggressive to give you a chance, but not so far out that it has little chance of succeeding. The important point to remember about risk and reward is that the reward part is only possible, not guaranteed. However, when you are right, you stand to make very high returns—you also have the opportunity to lose significantly. If you were to peg an age range for this type of portfolio, I would say 25 to 40 years old with the upper age range drifting into the moderate portfolio.

Here's how an aggressive portfolio might look (percentages are of your total invested capital):

Stocks—80 percent

Bonds—10 percent

Cash—10 percent

Within the stocks component, an investor could consider a mix of something like this:

Small-cap tech/growth stocks—25 percent

Core holdings—30 percent

Foreign stocks—15 percent

Mid-cap growth stocks—30 percent

Small-cap tech/growth stocks example. At the time I created this, one of the small tech/growth stocks considered was involved in providing software and services for the health-care industry, specifically electronic health-care records. The company faces competitors that are much bigger and better known, so the risks are high. However, if the company can hit a sweet spot with smaller health-care providers that may find some of the larger competitors intimidating to work with, it could see dramatic increases.

Core holdings example. The core holding is a household name, but many investors would be surprised to learn that most of its revenue comes from outside the United States. Its growth potential is in exploding markets such as China and India. Core holdings in an aggressive portfolio can have a sharper edge (more growth potential with very slight risk). This company will not grow as fast as predicted if global economic growth slows.

Foreign stock example. Foreign stocks are difficult to evaluate without a good service such as Morningstar. Their premium stock screener can be set for foreign stocks, although they must have a presence in the United States. Not surprisingly, many of the top-rated foreign stocks involved energy production and distribution. One Canadian example has large reserves tied up for exploration, and the future for continued high energy costs is good.

Mid-cap growth stock example. For this example, I chose a company in the video gaming industry. It is considered a market leader, but hasn't had a blockbuster hit recently. Investors concerned that it is no longer competitive in a very competitive market are concerned about the stock. However, with the company's resources and market presence, a new title could take off and the stock could soar.

STOCK TIP

While it is tempting to go "all in" with technology stocks in an aggressive portfolio, doing so subjects you to additional risks that the whole sector and all of your stocks could crater. There are good growth opportunities outside of technology.

A Moderate Portfolio

A moderate portfolio should target some stabilization in volatility; in other words, turn down the aggressive tactics in favor of a more moderate but predictable return. You still need growth to keep up and stay ahead of inflation and to push your return past the market's return. Bonds begin to play a larger role in the portfolio, again to add some stability. The moderate portfolio includes a larger presence for core stocks and a reduction in highly volatile small-cap issues. An age range for this portfolio might be 40 to 55 years old. I have included only one stock for each example, although it is reasonable to assume at this stage in life you may have the resources to own more than one issue in each category. Because most investors add to their holdings over a period, it is also reasonable that at some point in the process your percentages will be different from these (you may want to use different percentages when you are comfortable with your understanding of the selection process).

Here's how a moderate portfolio might look (percentages are of your total invested capital):

Stocks—60 percent

Bonds—30 percent

Cash—10 percent

Within the stocks component, an investor could consider a mix of something like this:

Large growth stocks—25 percent

Core holdings—45 percent

Foreign stocks—10 percent

Mid-cap value stocks—20 percent

Large growth stock example. The company I chose is dominant in the oil and gas service business with clients all over the world. Energy isn't getting any easier to find or recover, and this company will make money regardless of whether the resource is oil or gas and regardless of where the exploration is happening. No competitor is likely to capture much if any of its market share (very wide moat).

Core holdings example. Another household name, this company is a very diversified business with product lines in dozens of markets. They are market leaders in many of the industrial sectors where they compete, which gives them a balance that helps prevent peaks and valleys in price and returns. Note: this example is a cyclical company; it would be prudent to add a noncyclical stock to the core holdings.

Foreign stock example. I would stay with the same company I picked in the aggressive portfolio, but reduce its presence. Other foreign stocks would also work as long as they were in politically stable economies like our previous Canadian example.

Mid-cap value stock example. For-profit, post-secondary education has taken some hits in the media and before regulators (some well-deserved), yet this is an economic model that has long-term potential because it focuses on adults rather than young people just out of high school. Adult learners don't need, expect, or want dorms, sports teams, ivy-covered campuses, and so on. This gives this leader in for-profit education a real cost advantage over traditional colleges. Despite the beat-down over recruitment practices and less than strenuous academics, many for-profit colleges turn out well-educated adult graduates. This company is poised to rebound as the cost of traditional higher education continues to rise dramatically.

STOCK TIP

Value stocks are not substitutes for growth or core stocks, they are more like growth stocks waiting to happen. When they take off, value stocks can provide a good return.

A Conservative Portfolio

A conservative portfolio is primarily focused on capital preservation, which means reducing the exposure to the volatility of stocks and locking in principal in high-quality bonds and cash instruments. However, thanks to health-care advances, people are living longer, which means you must continue to risk some exposure to the stock market as a way to replenish the investment capital needed to convert to cash for living expenses. Persons aged 55 and up should begin transitioning into this portfolio no later than age 55 and be out of aggressive holdings completely by around age 60.

Here's how a conservative portfolio might look (percentages are of your total invested capital):

Stocks—30 percent

Bonds—50 percent

Cash—20 percent

Within the stocks component, an investor could consider a mix of something like this:

Core holdings noncyclical or defensive—55 percent

Core holdings cyclical—45 percent

Core holdings noncyclical or defensive example. I broke core holdings up into noncyclical and cyclical issues. For this example, I picked a large health-care company that makes a variety of name brand and generic pharmaceuticals in addition to over-the-counter products. Like most core holdings, it pays a strong dividend.

Core holdings cyclical example. I will use the previous example. Because it is slightly more prone to growth, it may help keep the portfolio above water if inflation returns.

Portfolio Lessons

The example portfolios are purely illustrations and subject to your own financial situation and tolerance for risk. I will say that the general philosophy of moving from aggressive to conservative as you grow older is one you should adopt. History tells us that the stock market can be extremely volatile in the short run and that it can be a disaster for a person near or in retirement if a substantial portion of his assets are in stocks. To make these (or any portfolio for that matter) work, you will also need to understand bonds, but that's another book.

Getting Started with a Stockbroker

>>> **In This Chapter**

- Learning the three types of stock brokerage firms
- Opening a brokerage account
- Learning the important stock market orders
- Keeping investing expenses low
- Having regulators that protect investors

This book is about long-term investing in stocks, not trading stocks on a frequent basis. Still, you will need a stockbroker to execute your orders to buy or sell. Navigating the world of stockbrokers can be confusing. There are several types of stock-brokerage firms offering a variety of services—some provide extensive help and recommendations while others simply process your order with no help or guidance on what you buy or sell. Hybrid companies offer a range of financial and broker services, depending on what you want and how much you have to invest. The firms range from "brick and mortar" to virtual online operations. All operate under the same basic set of regulations, although some types of firms have additional sets of rules. Which type of broker you use is a matter of personal taste and comfort. After you decide on a broker, you need to tell them what you want them to do. Stock market orders go way beyond buy and sell. An understanding of your options will help you make the best decisions. If you believe your broker has wronged you in some manner, there are safeguards built into the system (losing money on a trade usually doesn't count).

The World of Stockbrokers

The world of stockbrokers is dynamic if nothing else. What seems like just a few years ago, you could divide the pie into two basic pieces: full-service brokers and discount brokers (older readers may remember when there was only one type of stockbroker—full-service with big commissions). What really shook up the world of stockbrokers was the internet and the ability to perform brokerage services online. Prior to the mid-1990s, discount brokers took your order by phone or you went into their offices.

STOCK TIP

Online brokers are also discount brokers, but they lack physical offices where investors can drop by to place orders or ask questions. The lines between full-service brokers and discount brokers have blurred to the benefit of investors.

While it is still not always easy to fit each broker into a neat pigeonhole, you can make a general distinction by the services they offer with the understanding that most firms have broadened their range of services to touch on almost all aspects of the stock market experience. You will also find specialty brokers who focus in particular areas of the market, such as options, bonds, or other more sophisticated investment products. I won't cover them in this book, but be aware that they are out there and always looking for new customers.

Full-Service Brokers

At the top of the service provider list are full-service brokers. Full-service brokers today have to be much more than order takers (why use them otherwise?). Companies in this category profess to offer a complete range of financial advisory services that extend beyond picking stocks to retirement planning and meeting other financial goals.

The reason some investors turn to full-service brokers is for access to proprietary research on stocks and other financial instruments, along with the guidance of an investment professional. Many firms offer financial planning services that combine your investment accounts, retirement planning, and tax strategies. Full-service brokers maintain staffs that research and analyze stocks and bonds and offer proprietary analytical services that monitor your portfolio to minimize risk and maximize return.

Some full-service brokers also offer well-heeled investors the opportunity to participate in private offerings and provide access to hedge funds or other investments that are not generally available to the public. In many cases, to qualify for these services and products you will need a significant six-figure pool of capital for investment and have a very strong personal financial statement.

If you are uncomfortable making decisions about which stocks to buy or sell and want an experienced professional to help you, a full-service broker may be worth the large fees and commissions you will have to pay. The key to a successful relationship with a full-service broker is finding an individual within the company that you feel comfortable will put your interest before his or that of the company. The best way to find such an individual is by asking around and taking referrals from people you trust. Plan to meet with several brokers before making a decision so that the chemistry is right and you are comfortable with her experience and professionalism.

A good broker will listen to your goals and ask questions to determine what your level of risk is and suggest products that are appropriate for your financial situation, age, and goals. Industry ethics and rules prevent brokers from putting you in investments that are inappropriate for your financial situation. This doesn't mean it never happens.

Even at their most basic service level, full-service brokers can be expensive. Commissions that might run under $15 per trade otherwise could be several hundred dollars at a full-service broker.

Some full-service brokers prefer to work on a percentage of your invested assets as an annual fee. For this arrangement, they provide a menu of services. It is important that you have a complete understanding of what is included in all fees and commissions so there's no misunderstanding at a later date.

The pros of full-service brokers:

- Offer professional help building your portfolio
- Access to proprietary research and products
- Can look at the total financial picture including retirement planning and tax strategies

Full-service broker cons:

- High fees for services
- Compensation may encourage excessive trading
- May push proprietary products that are not the best choice

Discount Brokers

Today's discount broker has evolved into more than an order taker. There is a big slice of the market that wants something more than an order taker, but less than the handholding of a full-service broker. Many of these brokers offer investment advice, but short of the comprehensive planning you might get with a full-service broker. They may have excellent research resources available on their websites and robust online capabilities.

Discount brokers and their close cousins, online brokers, offer many of the same services, so choosing between the two may be based on other factors. Many of the leading discount brokers now offer a variety of services that were once the domain of full-service brokers. However, in most cases they do not offer investment advice. While some discount brokers may offer you the opportunity to speak directly with a broker who can at least offer some opinions on your decision, this will come at a higher price than their normal trade fee.

In the past, some discount brokers were merely phone banks who took your order over the phone and then emailed it to a third-party for actual execution. If you stick with well-known discount brokers, this is not likely to happen. In addition, some discount brokers have offices around the country where you can go to set up an account or place an order. Some discount brokers offer access to research, which may come from a third party. This is not a bad alternative if you want more detailed information than is readily available for free over the internet.

Discount brokers still take phone orders and many also offer online services if you're more comfortable with that type of interface or if you are somewhere that a phone call is not practical. With the proliferation of smart phones and tablets, discount brokers offer apps that let you transact business on the go.

 MARKET RISK

If you decide to use a smart phone to place orders and do other investing business, be sure you are comfortable with the security of your information. Ask the broker what systems are in place to secure the transaction.

As with all brokers, it is important that you thoroughly understand the fees and commissions you will pay and when extras cost over and above the regular fees (more about this in the later section on stock orders). This should all be clearly explained on the company's website, or if you visit in person you should be given a complete list of fees and commissions. Be especially careful about minimum deposits or account balances the company may require. If your balance drops below this minimum, you may be paying either a monthly service fee or higher charges on your trades.

Another area to consider is how much interest, if any, the broker will pay when you have cash in your account. For example, if you sell a stock, the money stays in your account until you tell the broker what to do with it. In some cases, you will want to reinvest it in the near future, which means it's probably a better idea to simply leave it in the account rather than transfer it back and forth from the broker to you and you back to the broker when you are ready for your next buy. Some brokers may pay you interest on the money while it is waiting to be reinvested. This is not a deal breaker in most cases, because if you don't plan to reinvest the cash soon, it's better to take the money out of the brokerage account and put it somewhere else that pays more interest.

It's a good idea to visit the discount broker's website and become familiar with how they do business online. In some cases, the discount broker's website may let you open a practice account where you can buy and sell stocks using fake money so you can become familiar with the software and how it works. If not, most discount brokers offer tutorials and even lessons on investing that may be helpful.

Long-term investors are usually not very active accounts for discount brokerages. You may not qualify for any special deals on commissions because you make only a few trades per year. The difference of a few dollars per trade is inconsequential when you seldom use the service. What is more important is how easy it is to access your account and make an order. For my money, you should be able to access your account by phone, by smart phone, by the web, or by walking into an office and talking to a real person.

The pros of discount brokers:

- May offer the same services as full-service brokers without high fees
- Usually don't require a high initial deposit
- Can access your account in person, by phone, by smart phone, or online

Discount broker cons:

- May charge extra for all but basic services
- No fee breaks for infrequent traders
- Watch for minimum balance requirements

STOCK TIP

It is important to keep expenses down when investing, but don't be too cheap and pick a broker that lacks the tools and connections you need to feel comfortable with your trades.

Online Brokers

Online brokers offer many of the same services that discount brokers do, though of course without physical offices. Most of the transactions they process come through their website, which may have a variety of options for you to consider. For example, some online brokers offer third-party research or other investment tools, such as portfolio monitors and price alerts if those are important to you.

While some online brokers will process phone orders, that is not their preferred method of communication. If you are comfortable working online and dealing with services over the web, this may not be an issue. However, what happens if you lose your internet connection or you happen to be somewhere your smart phone doesn't have a signal and you need to place an order with your online broker? Also, there have been times during heavy market activity when some online brokers have had difficulty keeping up with incoming volume, which may mean their website is unavailable, perhaps at the time when you need it the most.

As a rule, online brokers may offer the best rates and faster service in processing your orders. However, you could also say the same thing about many discount brokers. Squeezing a few dollars off commissions is less important than the confidence that your order will be accepted and executed in a timely and correct manner. There are some people who would much rather deal with an online service than another human. If that's you, an online broker or a discount broker may make perfect sense.

With online brokers, it is especially important that they have prompt and reliable customer service, whether you reach them over the phone or online. It is a given that in the middle of an important transaction something will happen and you will need help resolving the matter. There's nothing worse than not knowing if your order has been accepted or not when the market is extremely volatile.

The pros of online brokers:

- Usually lowest commissions
- Quick execution with no upselling of products
- May offer some online tools with service

Online broker cons:

- Customer service can be an issue
- Problems if website is unavailable
- Virtually no help or guidance

Which Broker Type Is Right for You?

Picking a broker shouldn't be about price alone. Be honest with yourself about how much help you can use and go with the broker who can fill in any gaps in your knowledge and experience. The clearest distinction between broker types is full service and every other type of broker. When you begin comparing discount brokers and online brokers, you may find it hard to tell the difference between the two. Indeed, you could conclude that slotting every broker into only one of these types is not practical or useful.

When you know what you want from your broker, visit different websites and see if there is a good fit. If you have access to a discount broker's physical office, make an appointment and visit with a representative. If you stay with one of the major brokerages, you can be comfortable that they will take care of your business in a prompt and ethical manner. If they don't, I have a process you can use to have your complaint heard. In most cases, a visit with a supervisor can clear up many problems. Brokers live by referrals of satisfied customers and will go to great lengths to avoid bad word-of-mouth comments. Thanks to social media, those complaints can spread rapidly and widely.

Opening a Brokerage Account

Before you can begin trading stocks, you must open an account with your broker. Depending on what type of broker you choose, opening an account can range from a very personal to very impersonal process. There are several different types of accounts that most brokers offer in addition to the level of service you receive from the different types of brokers. First, I go over how the two basic types of brokers set up accounts and then I describe the different types of accounts.

STOCK TIP

Be prepared with your Social Security number, bank account information, and a form of photo identification to open any brokerage account. You may need to fax documents to an online broker's main office before they will open an account.

Full-Service Broker Accounts

A full-service broker will want to sit down with you and your spouse or partner and go over your financial situation in some detail. He will want to know about any debts, cash in the bank, any stock or mutual funds you own, retirement plans, insurance, home ownership, kids, your income, and so forth.

They are required to gather this information before they can make recommendations to you regarding investments. In the business, it's called "know your customer." If a broker makes an inappropriate investment recommendation to someone because he or she did not take the time to find out all about the customer's financial circumstances, the broker can face severe penalties. This is one of the services you buy with the commissions you pay to a full-service broker—recommendations that are appropriate for your individual financial situation. Many investors consider it money well spent.

Discount/Online Brokers Accounts

Discount and online brokers offer no advice and make no recommendations; therefore, setting up accounts with them is far less personal. There are still forms to fill out and questions to answer, but no one is going to come to your house and look at your checkbook. You are on your own in determining if the stock is right for you. Some particular types of investment (options, futures, and other high-risk investments) require you to certify that you are a knowledgeable investor, able to understand the risks associated with the product.

However, regulators are very particular about what might constitute a "recommendation" to buy or sell. If a broker in any way suggests, hints, or recommends a customer buy or sell a particular security, that constitutes a recommendation and the broker must have the necessary "know your customer" forms on file. If an online or discount broker provides you access to research, but doesn't suggest a particular security and you have the ability to research any security you want, that does not qualify as a recommendation. If a discount broker offers you the opportunity to talk with an investment professional, you will probably need to fill out the detailed questionnaire.

Types of Accounts

There are several types of accounts that most brokers offer. They include ...

- Cash accounts
- Margin accounts
- Discretionary accounts

There may be others that are particular to individual brokerages, but they will be variations of one of these three.

Cash Accounts

A cash account is the simplest type of brokerage account and the first one you will probably open. Online and discount brokers will most likely require you to make a deposit with enough money to cover your trade before they will open your account. Many will place this money in an interest-bearing account until you are ready to trade. When you place a buy order, the broker transfers the money to the brokerage account to cover the trade. When you sell a stock, the broker will deposit the proceeds in the account (unless you instruct them otherwise), so cash is available for the next purchase.

With a full-service broker, you may have three days to pay for your purchase, depending on the broker's policy. However, many will also want money deposited in the account before trading begins. Trades must be paid for or "settled" within three days. This is called the "settlement date" and if you are a good customer with good credit, a full-service broker will give you those days to pay.

Margin Accounts

Margin accounts allow you to borrow money from the broker to buy stocks. A margin account allows you to borrow up to 50 percent of the value of the stock from your broker when you make a purchase. For example, if you want to buy $10,000 of stock, you could write a check for $10,000 or with a margin account, write a check for $5,000, and borrow $5,000 from your broker. Obviously, these accounts require more documentation and a stellar credit rating.

By borrowing one-half the value of the stock, you can multiply your profits dramatically. Here's how that works: if the price of the stock doubles to $20,000, your investment in the margin account ($5,000) increases four-fold. You sell the stock and pay the broker back the $5,000 you borrowed. Your $5,000 has earned $10,000. If you paid cash for the stock ($10,000), you would have earned the same $10,000, but on a $10,000 investment.

With a margin account, you can make your money work harder if you own more stock. However, there is risk. If the value of the stock falls instead of rises, your broker will issue a "margin call." A margin call usually comes when the value of the stock falls below the value of the money lent to you by the broker. However, some brokers may have different thresholds for margin calls. When you get a margin call, you have two options: you can deposit cash into the account to raise the value above the amount you borrowed or you can sell the stock immediately and pay off the loan. Some brokers may not give you the option of depositing cash; they may liquidate your position for you when the stock falls below a certain price.

MARKET RISK

Trading on margin has appeal and when it works in your favor, it's a wise move. However, don't get excited with the prospect of "easy money"—speculation is a game you will lose.

Discretionary Accounts

Discretionary accounts give a broker or financial adviser the right to buy and sell stock without notifying you. If a broker wants this authorization, go find another broker. Unless you trust a broker or financial adviser with your life, never give anyone this type of control over your finances—it is the equivalent of a blank check. There are circumstances when these types of accounts are appropriate; however, for most of us they are not only inappropriate, but also hazardous to our financial well-being.

Stock Market Orders You Should Know

The world of buying and selling stocks has its own language, which may sound confusing, but fortunately long-term investors need only master a few of the basic orders. You will communicate your orders to your broker by whatever method is appropriate, whether in person, over the phone, or online. The orders are industry standard and there shouldn't be much variation among different brokers. It is important that you know what happens when each type of order is executed so there will be no unpleasant surprises.

The basic orders are to buy or sell, however it is a bit more complicated than that. You need to specify what type of buy or sell order you want. Here are the stock market orders you need to know.

Market Orders

The market order is the simplest and quickest way to get your order filled (or completed). A market order instructs your broker to buy or sell the stock immediately at the prevailing price, whatever that may be. If you are following the market, you may or may not get the last price listed. In a volatile market, you will probably get a price close to that, but there is no guarantee of any specific price. Unless you have access to real-time quotes, either through your broker or some other service, the prices you see on most web pages are delayed by 20 minutes. Twenty minutes can be a lifetime in a volatile stock market.

In many cases, the stock's price may not be bouncing around that much and you don't care if you pay or receive $0.25 per share one way or the other. Still, you are taking a chance on the price and that is usually not a good idea unless you have to sell and don't care. One final, but important note: market orders will likely be the most inexpensive of the orders you place.

Limit Orders

Limit orders instruct your broker to buy or sell a stock at a particular price. The purchase or sale will not happen unless you get your price. Limit orders give you control over your entry or exit point by fixing the price, which can be helpful. Limit orders are your best choice in most cases. For example, if you have decided that you want to buy Stock A at no more than $25 per share and it is currently trading at $27 per share, you could put a limit buy order in for $25 per share. If the stock drops to that point, your order will be executed. Note that if the price drops through your price you may still pay the $25 per share because the market takes the best orders first. The same process works for limit sell orders. If you will sell at a price above or below the current market price (to protect a profit or cut a loss), a limit buy order is appropriate (see stop-loss orders next).

Check with your broker to see how the commission on limit orders compares with what you pay for market orders. If there is a significant difference, you may be better off with a market order (assuming the price is at or near your target) and saving on commissions. In most cases, though, it is still advisable to have a price with your order.

Stop-Loss Orders

A stop-loss order gives your broker a price trigger that protects you from a big drop in a stock. You enter a stop-loss order at a point below the current market price. If the stock falls to this price point, the stop-loss order becomes a market order and your broker sells the stock. If the stock stays level or rises, the stop-loss order does nothing. Stop-loss orders are cheap insurance that protects you from a loss.

Trailing Stops

The trailing stop order is similar to the stop-loss order, but you use it to protect a profit, as opposed to protect against a loss. If you have a profit in a stock, you can use the trailing stop order to follow it up in price. You enter the trailing stop order as a percentage of the market price. If the stock continues to rise, the trailing stop follows it up because it is a percentage of the market price. This protects your additional gains. If the market price declines by that percentage, the trailing stop becomes a market order and your broker sells the stock. For long-term investors, trailing stops are for stocks you want to sell, but want to let them rise in price as long as possible. When the price retreats, the trailing stop kicks in and you are out of the stock with your profit.

MARKET RISK

If you use an online system that lets you enter your trades without the assistance of a human, make certain you understand what you are doing, because there may be order options available that you are unfamiliar with.

Placing an Order with Your Broker

A limit order, whether given to a stockbroker or entered into an online system, has the same five components:

- Buy or sell
- Number of shares
- Security
- Order type
- Price

For example, if you wanted to buy 100 shares of XYZ using a limit order, here's how you would express it:

Buy 100 shares of XYZ: limit 33.45

This order tells the market you will buy 100 shares of XYZ, but under no circumstances will you pay more than $33.45 per share.

STOCK TIP

It will take some experience to know where to set limit orders. If you set limit buy orders too low they may never be filled, which does you no good. The same is true for limit sell orders. With some experience you'll find the spot that gets you a good price and your order filled.

How to Keep Investing Expenses Low

The expenses of investing in the stock market can cut into your returns if you are not careful. I already discussed taxes in Chapter 8, which are a major expense if you do not properly time your transactions. Another obvious expense is the cost of doing business with a broker. There are commissions, fees, and other costs (such as extra fees for limit orders). Beyond that, you can rack up plenty of extra expenses that may pay for services or products you don't need. Here are some of the more common expenses:

Research and analysis. There are hundreds of research services on the web that range from free or inexpensive to outrageous. I have already noted that the premium features of Morningstar are worth the modest fee. Other offerings may cost hundreds of dollars per month. Some are delivered via email, while others come from in-person seminars often at lavish resorts. Be very careful about what you pay for in investing research and analysis.

Investing or trading systems. Every day, at least it seems that way, someone else comes up with a "revolutionary" system that promises triple-digit returns and all types of unbelievable success if you just use their simple system. Not likely.

Hardware/software. You do not need expensive hardware (computers) or software to be successful as a long-term investor. Any relatively new computer will be perfectly adequate and the software you need is available from your broker over the web. If you plan to do a lot of research online (I highly recommend it), consider a broadband (high speed) internet connection if you don't already have the service. Your local cable company or phone provider can usually hook you up.

Publications/newsletters. There are some good paid subscription publications and newsletters for interested investors. However, there are an equal or greater number for free online. Whether you are considering a paid or free publication, be sure you understand what if anything the publisher has to gain (do they sell financial products and could the content direct you toward a purchase?).

MARKET RISK

A popular ploy is to offer a seminar on investing at a luxury resort and suggest that you can write off the cost as an investment expense. Never take tax advice from someone who has something to gain if you follow the advice.

What You Do When Things Go Badly

As an investor, you have certain rights that your broker must acknowledge. As previously noted, brokers have a legal and ethical responsibility to deal with you fairly and appropriately. Unfortunately, like any business, stock brokers sometimes bend or break the rules. It is somewhat disconcerting to read about the actions of some financial firms during the financial collapse of 2008 and stories of misdeed on a much smaller scale abound.

Despite the unfortunate headlines, the securities industry is one of the most highly regulated businesses in the United States. The U.S. Congress is at the top of the heap. It created most of the structure and it passes major laws that affect how the industry operates. It also authorizes budgets for the Securities and Exchange Commission (SEC) and other agencies involved in regulatory duties. The SEC is the top regulatory agency responsible for overseeing the securities industry. It registers new securities and handles all the filings that public companies must make, such as annual and quarterly reports.

The SEC

The SEC also oversees all of the stock exchanges and any organization connected with the selling of securities. It also has a strong anti-fraud unit that monitors advertising and marketing to make sure companies comply with strict rules concerning the sale of securities. You can find all of the public filings (financial statements and so on) on the SEC's website.

Financial Industry Regulatory Authority (FINRA)

At the next level is the Financial Industry Regulatory Authority (FINRA). It was created in 2007 when the National Association of Securities Dealers merged with the regulatory functions of the New York Stock Exchange. This is an industry self-regulatory body that is responsible for policing the securities industry. FINRA set standards for stockbrokers and other industry professionals and licenses them after comprehensive examinations.

FINRA has the ability to fine individuals and organizations for unethical behavior and can revoke licenses. The organization is usually the place customers can take complaints of behavior they feel is unethical or illegal. FINRA also monitors trading activities of member firms to detect illegal trading patterns and other illegal activity. The individual exchanges also have sophisticated regulatory oversight functions within their own operations. These include monitoring trades and other steps to see that the customer gets a fair deal. Search for FINRA on the web for the nearest office and how to file a complaint.

Individual States

Individual states also have securities divisions, although they are usually not as sophisticated as FINRA. Often they handle complaints and register securities that will be sold within the boundaries of the state, although this will vary from state to state. You can find contact information for your state's security regulation departments at http://www.nasaa.org/about-us/contact-us/contact-your-regulator/.

Broker's In-House Monitoring

The final step of protection (or the first in order of where you should start) is at the brokerage level. Each firm is required to keep certain records and perform certain checks and audits of the operation to make sure their brokers are operating within acceptable legal and ethical guidelines. If you have a problem, contact the managing broker. Many problems can be solved at this level.

Mistakes to Avoid and Tools to Use

One of the best ways to make money in the stock market is to avoid losing it. No one wants to lose money, but the reality of investing dictates that you will lose money on a stock you buy. There is no foolproof way to only pick winners. Investors can, however, avoid common mistakes that will cost them money no matter how well they pick stocks. In every case, investors create problems by failing to act, acting emotionally, or ignoring the facts. You can prevent these mistakes and avoid losing money if you know where the traps are in investing.

Any task is easier if you have the right tools, and investing is no different. Thankfully, most of the tools available to you are easy to access and they can help simplify the process and mechanics of investing.

Common Investing Mistakes and How to Avoid Them

We all make mistakes, but there are some that we can avoid if we know what they are beforehand. Investing in stocks, like anything involving money, is an emotion-laden experience. For some investors, it is easy to put the anxieties aside and focus on the facts. For others, money is more complicated and dodging the emotional mine fields is more difficult. Where you fall on this spectrum may make it easier or harder to avoid mistakes. Even those investors with difficult relations with money can avoid mistakes if they see them coming. The following mistakes can trip up anyone, so be forewarned.

Playing Catch-Up

One of the most common problems investors in the stock market face is trying to catch up for the years they missed contributing to a retirement plan. With millions of baby boomers approaching retirement, panic has set in among those who have not adequately planned for how they will fund their retirement. In some cases, pensions were wiped out when companies went bankrupt, people were unemployed for significant periods of time, or they generally just did not think far enough ahead to put money away for retirement.

As these investors approach middle age, they panic when they realize all the years they missed investing in their retirement. They instead chose to do something else with their money or simply did not have the money to spare. The common solution is to make the most aggressive choices they can in hopes of picking winning stocks that will do so well they make up for 20 years of inactivity.

The problem here of course is that making excessively risky bets on the stock market almost always ends poorly. High-risk investments mean that many if not all of them will fail to achieve expected results and may in fact come crashing down.

You can't make up for decades of inactivity by becoming hyperactive in middle age or later. The obvious mistake here is making risky bets, which have little chance of success. So, what is a middle-aged person to do when they realize they have few if any assets put away for retirement? In most cases, their best bet is to follow a commonsense strategy to build the retirement fund as rapidly and responsibly as they can. Here are some steps they can take:

Review your budget. Take a hard look at your budget and begin cutting as many luxuries as you can out of your monthly spending. Don't buy a new car every couple of years; drop expensive club memberships if you use them infrequently; skip the vacation to Europe and stay closer to home; then review other steps you can take to save money in other ways, as well.

STOCK TIP

Your money grows through compounding. Compounding is made up of three components: amount invested, time for compounding, and rate of return. If you have not saved for retirement in the past, boost the amount you invest, but avoid shooting for an abnormally high rate of return—that doesn't work.

Retirement plan. If you work for an employer with a retirement plan, such as a 401(k), increase your participation by as much as possible. There are limits on how much you can contribute and your human resources department can explain those to you.

Additional cash. Any additional cash you can find should go into an appropriate investment model portfolio for your financial situation and time remaining to retirement. Rather than invest in high-risk stocks, keep your investments inline with what's appropriate for your age. At this point you cannot afford to take huge losses on risky investments.

Fall in Love with a Stock or a Company

I am a big fan of Apple products. For me, they provide extremely functional experiences with style and sophistication. I wish I had spent as much time analyzing Apple stock as I did following its products. The stock was dirt-cheap in the early 2000s compared to 10 years later. As it turned out, Apple would have been a great buy; however, buying Apple stock because I loved its products would have been a mistake. Anyone remember VHS tapes or audiocassette tapes? I have boxes of both sitting in my basement and they are essentially worthless. I loved those, too.

It is too bad that I didn't invest in Apple stock, but it points out a mistake that many people make. Whether Apple stock is going to continue its dramatic rise is the subject of much debate among stock market analysts and investors. If I decide to buy Apple stock, it will be based on my research that indicates it still has much room to climb. It will not be based on the fact that I'm a big fan of their products.

It seems like every week there is a new company that is a darling of the stock market. Investors who do not look beyond the hype and media attention and buy the stock based on the excitement factor may have a rude awakening when the company's fundamentals don't live up to its image. This is not to say that a popular company can't also be a good investment. The key is to look for financial strength—a wide economic moat, and all of the other factors that make a great company, are discussed in earlier chapters.

Once in the recent past, a company named Enron was a media darling and the high-flying stock that charmed the investing public. Company executives encouraged employees to put all of their 401(k) contributions into Enron stock. When it came to light that company officials were manipulating the financial information they reported to stockholders and the SEC, the company stock went into a nosedive. In the end, the company was bankrupt and all the stockholders lost everything. The real tragedy was that the company's employees, who had no idea of the fraud, had their retirement savings wiped out when the stock became worthless.

The mistake here is not looking at every company you are considering investing in through the same logical process regardless of how much you like the company or how much the media and investment community loves the company. A good public relations campaign is no substitute for a financially healthy and well-run company. Great companies demonstrate their worth in their financial statements, economic moat, and the other factors used to analyze its health.

The investment landscape is littered with companies that have had their moment in the sun but failed at a fundamental business level or were tied to an industry or consumer segment that was not growing or was saturated with competitors.

 MARKET RISK

Some companies fail because of fraud, but most fail because management does not adapt to changing markets and business realities. Fax machines were once the rage. Now, most have been replaced by email and other online communication options.

Market Timing

Market timing may be the two most dangerous words in investing. Timing the market is about buying a stock just before it begins a rapid move upward. Almost everyone who's been involved in the stock market at one time or another has seen opportunities they are convinced will make them a large sum of money because somehow they have predicted the future price of a stock or stock market indexes. After the fact, they can do what I did with Apple stock and say if only I had bought that stock on this date, I would be a rich person now. Of course, everyone is great at looking at the stock market through the rearview mirror and picking winners.

The mistake comes when investors convince themselves that they can predict a winner before it happens. It is called timing the market because investors convince themselves that if they buy now it will just precede a huge increase that will make them rich. To set the record straight, there is no system, no software, no technique, and no crystal ball that will tell you with any consistency which way the market is moving. Yet, you will see dozens if not hundreds of systems, strategies, software, or whatever that claim to do exactly this. A mistake many investors make is to abandon their research and go with a hot tip or gut feeling. It is even possible that once or twice you may guess correctly; however, the 8 or 10 other times you guess and are wrong will outweigh any gains you make on your correct guess.

You should ask yourself: Do I want to bet my retirement or my kids' college education on a guess? The strategies I have outlined in this book are time-tested and proven: identify great companies, buy them at a great price, and hold on for the long term. This buy-and-hold strategy has its detractors, most of whom are convinced they have a system they would love to sell you. They claim that their market timing system will pull you out of the market before it collapses and get you back in when it begins its ascent. They charge that buy-and-hold investors watch their account value drop along with the market when they could avoid those drops if they only used this system.

The best response to their allegations is to point to Warren Buffett, who is acknowledged as the most successful investor of all time. His investment strategy remained consistent throughout his career, and that was to buy great companies at great prices and let them build wealth for over the years.

Abandoning Your Plan When the Market Drops

One of the classic mistakes investors make is to abandon their investment plan when the market goes into a deep dive. Ask any stockbroker what happens when the market takes a nosedive, and almost every one of them will tell you that their phone won't stop ringing from clients who want to cash out of the stock market. These are the same clients the broker has convinced to adopt a strategy of buying great companies at great prices and holding them while they create wealth.

As previously noted, money is a very emotional topic and the fear of loss is the strongest emotion of all. It is difficult and painful to watch the value of your portfolio follow the market down into what may seem like a bottomless pit. The first reaction of many investors is to simply sell everything and take their money out of the stock market. That is almost always exactly the wrong thing to do. How should an investor react when the market is on one of its rollercoaster rides that happen to be pointing down at this time?

For making a decision under any circumstances, the first step is to re-examine the companies you own to verify they still fit into your overall investment plan. If something has fundamentally changed about the company—for example, they have lost their economic advantage or have become financially unstable—you should seriously consider selling the stock regardless of what the stock market is doing.

One of the few things we know for certain about the stock market is that it will go up and it will go down. However, no one has a clear idea when either of these events is going to happen. The strategy I've outlined in this book will protect you as much as possible during those times when the stock market is going down and it will create the opportunity for growth when the market is going up. When you are approaching retirement, it is important to begin moving your money out of stocks and into bonds and cash. This way market rollercoasters will not devastate your assets at a time when you need them most, such as the one that began in 2008 and saw a drop of some 50 percent, but rebounded by 2012. For all other investors, the best strategy after re-evaluating all of the companies and confirming they still meet the qualifications you needed when you bought them is to remain in the market and let your great companies do what they do best.

When the market rebounds, you will be there with your great companies to participate in the recovery.

STOCK TIP

Remember, the daily stock market gyrations have nothing to do with the value a company creates. Over time, great companies create wealth through consistent profits and, in many cases, dividends.

Rules Have Changed

This mistake is sometimes known as "the rules are different this time." The problem with this mistake, like a lot of the stuff you hear about the stock market, is that it is never different this time or any time and the important rules never change. Yet every time we see a bubble in the stock market, the know-it-alls trout the same tired and wrong pronouncements. During the dot. com boom, it was the "new economy" or the "web economy" that excited the market—the old rules didn't apply anymore. In March 2000, the Nasdaq Composite closed at just more than 5,000. That same month, market historians discovered that the dot.com bubble burst. The Nasdaq bottomed out at 1,100—a staggering 78 percent loss. By early 2012, 12 years after the disaster, the index climbed higher than 3,000 for the first time.

In retrospect, the cause of the burst was clear: traders bid up any tech stock that had anything to do with the internet, which was now being discovered by the public as something very useful and not a gadget for geeks. Ultimately, the market always corrects to valuation. If a stock has the numbers behind it, it will continue a growth trend. Value investors count on the market correcting to value, because when that happens the underpriced stock they bought will take off.

Some Other Investing Mistakes

The following are some of the other classic mistakes investors make when they let their fear or greed overrule their plan:

Hot tips. Acting on hot tips is almost always a recipe for over-paying. By the time you hear about a "hot tip," the professional traders have bought and sold the stock and made their profit. You will buy at the top of an inflated price that will almost certainly fall well below what you paid.

Forgetting trading costs. It's easy to forget that it costs money now and in the future to make a profit on a stock trade. In the present, there is a commission to pay; in the future, you will pay a commission when you sell and taxes on any profits. Which taxes you pay will depend on how long you held the stock before you sold it. A stock must rise enough in price to cover all the past trading costs, future trading costs, and the anticipated taxes, and still have a nice profit for you.

Poor diversification. If you fail to properly diversify your hold-ings, you're setting yourself up for a major setback. An economic move can cause an across-the-board drop in price if you are not diversified. Diversification lowers your risk by spreading your investing dollars over industries and asset classes. As you are building a portfolio, you may not have the resources to achieve good diversification quickly. In the interim, buy a low-cost market index fund or exchange traded fund to help with diversifi-cation (see the following).

Speculating. Investors can easily forget they are investing for the long term and be lured into the excitement of trading for the short term. Traders buy and sell stocks over short periods: seconds, minutes, hours, days, weeks. It takes a great deal of experience and nerve to be an active trader. Most long-term investors don't have the experience or risk tolerance for speculat-ing and are lured into trading by the potential for gain, only to find it is hard work and an easy way to lose money.

Inability to sell. Investors sometimes have a difficult time admitting to themselves that an investment isn't working out. They hold on irrationally, hoping the company is going to bounce back from the brink of bankruptcy. Investors should set a loss limit and sell when the stock hits that mark.

Giving up too soon. Investing in stocks is a long-term commitment—at least five years or more. Even companies with good fundamental economics may stall in price. If you had a logical reason for investing in the company in the first place, be patient and let the market catch up with your thinking.

Index

Numbers

A

B

S

W–X–Y–Z

weaknesses, discounted cash
  flows, 75
web economy, 132
websites
    Forbes.com, 29
    Morningstar, 26-27
    MSN Money, 29
    stock screens, 31-34
    Stocks About.com, 30
    The Street, 29
    Yahoo! Finance, 27-29

Yahoo! Finance, 27-29